THE
MEATH
WAR DEAD

THE
MEATH
WAR DEAD

A HISTORY OF THE CASUALTIES OF THE GREAT WAR

NOEL FRENCH

First published 2011

The History Press Ireland
119 Lower Baggot Street
Dublin 2, Ireland
www.thehistorypress.ie

© Noel French, 2011

The right of Noel French to be identified as the Author
of this work has been asserted in accordance with the
Copyrights, Designs and Patents Act 1988.

British Library Cataloguing in Publication Data.
A catalogue record for this book is available from the British Library.

ISBN 978 1 84588 723 0
Typesetting and origination by The History Press
Printed in Great Britain

Contents

Introduction   7

A–Z List of Meath War Dead

A   9
B   11
C   18
D   35
E   44
F   45
G   51
H   59
I   67
J   68
K   69
L   74
M   82
N   105
O   107
P   112
Q   118
R   119
S   130
T   136
V   139
W   140
Y   144

Casualties Broken Down by Area   145
Sources and Further Information   155

It is too late now to retrieve
A fallen dream, too late to grieve
A name unmade, but not too late
To thank the gods for what is great;
A keen-edged sword, a soldier's heart,
Is greater than a poet's art.
And greater than a poet's fame
A little grave that has no name.

Francis Ledwidge

Introduction

The objective of this book is to record and remember the names of the Meath men who lost their lives fighting in the Great War, 1914–1918.

These men were not just statistics; each was an individual living human being. Not only are the dates and places of deaths of each man recorded but the author attempts to give some background details including parents, dates of baptisms, occupations of their parents and their own occupations.

As a result of the war 500 men from Meath lie in graveyards from Basra to Bermuda, from Jerusalem to Gallipoli, from Ypres to Teltown and everywhere in between.

This list has been compiled from various sources and I would like to particularly acknowledge the recent works by Michael McGoona and Donal Hall.

Included in the list are all who were born in Meath; who were living in Meath when they enlisted; or had parents, wives, or primary family in the county, and those commemorated in memorials in the county.

Stained-glass window, St Patrick's church, Slane.

Some addresses are misspelled in the original sources. These have been corrected where possible but in cases where it is unclear, the spellings have been left as they were in the original documents. Caution should be exercised in using the addresses given in the records as sometimes these are temporary or accommodation addresses.

When searching through the names please do search variant spelling such as 'Smith' and 'Smyth' and 'McGuire' and 'Maguire' as the spelling of names in the records can vary. Not all information is completely accurate. Some sources give conflicting information and some information is speculative. There are sometimes differing details with regard to battalions, dates of death and other details. In some cases different versions have been left and in other cases the records appear as they do in the majority of the sources.

The term 'France & Flanders' includes all French and Belgian battlefields. 'Home' can mean at their own house or in Ireland or Britain and sometimes a hospital in Britain or Ireland.

For some individuals there was not sufficient information to make a definite connection to a baptism or census entry. There may have been no information or conflicting information.

The men who enlisted were Roman Catholic, Church of Ireland and Presbyterian. Baptism records come from the Catholic and Church of Ireland parish records.

I have only recorded the deaths up to the end of 1919. There were additional deaths in the 1920s as a result of injuries received in the War.

Some men documented were born in the county but their families were not long residing in the county and may have moved on before the men signed up for war. Some Meath families emigrated to England, Wales, Scotland, Canada and Australia and the men enlisted there.

The list is incomplete due to the difficulty of tracing men who enlisted in Australia, Canada and America. Records for the Royal Navy have also been difficult to source.

The breakdown by district is approximate and does not include all the entries.

I would like to thank Tom French, Local Studies Section, Meath County Library; Commonwealth War Graves Commission; the staff of the Meath Heritage Centre and in particular Maura Maguire, Carmel Rice, John McManus and Lesley Whiteside; The King's Hospital, Palmerstown; Andrew Whiteside, Philip Cantwell, O'Dare family, Oliver Fallon, Connaught Rangers, Tadhg Moloney, Royal Munster Fusiliers Association, Terence Nelson, Royal Irish Rifles, Geoffrey J. Crump, Cheshire Regimental Museum, *Meath Chronicle*, Meath County Library and all the other people who contributed to this book.

Noel French, 2011

A

AHEARNE, Michael James: Seaman, Royal Naval Reserve, HMS *Viknor*. Baptised: St Mary's, Drogheda, 24 May 1894. Son of David J. and Teresa Ahearne, *née* Connell, Woodside, Bettystown, Drogheda. Father's occupation: Wine and Spirit Merchant. Drowned, 13 January 1915, vessel lost off Irish coast. Memorial: M.R.3, Portsmouth Naval Memorial.

ALLEN, John: Private, Royal Irish Fusiliers, 1st Battalion, 16754. Born: Trim. Enlistment location: Dublin. Died: France & Flanders, 25 November 1916. Memorial: B.37, Fillievres British Cemetery. Drogheda War Memorial.

ALLEN, Patrick Christopher: Able Seaman, Royal Navy, HMS *Arabis*, 181318. Son of James and Bridget Allen, *née* Rice, Mooretown, Dunshaughlin. Killed in action, with T.B.D. in North Sea, 11 February 1916. Age: 40. Memorial: 11, Plymouth Naval Memorial.

ARMSTRONG, John: Private, Royal Inniskilling Fusiliers, 2nd Battalion, 10665. Born: Lisburn, Co. Antrim. Son of William and Kate Armstrong, Lower Fennor, Oldcastle. Brother, William, also killed in the war. Residence: Oldcastle. Enlistment location: Dublin. Served in France from 24 November 1915. Killed in action, France & Flanders, 16 May 1915. Age: 17. Memorial: Panel 16 and 17, Le Touret Memorial.

ARMSTRONG, William M.: Acting Sergeant, Royal Inniskilling Fusiliers, 7/8th Battalion, 9614. Son of William and Kate Armstrong, Lower Fennor, Oldcastle. Brother, John, also killed in the war. Husband of Mary Armstrong, *née* Newman, Knockshangan, Athboy. Enlistment location: Finner Camp, Co. Donegal. Killed in action, France & Flanders, 22 August 1917. Age: 28. Awards: Military Medal. Memorial: XI.C.3, Harlebeke New British Cemetery. From the *Meath Chronicle*, 26 May 1917, 'Lance-Corporal Wm. Armstrong, Inniskilling Fusiliers, a native of Oldcastle, in a letter to his sister states he won two boxing contests – a heavy and middle-weight, out in France.'

AUGHEY, John: Corporal, Royal Irish Regiment, 2nd Battalion, 9542. Baptised Kells, 7 January 1886. Son of John and Catherine Aughey, *née* Smith. Brother, Owen, also killed in the war. Enlistment location: Rochdale, Lancashire. Served in France from 13 August 1914. Killed in action, France & Flanders, 21 March 1918. Memorial: Panel 30 and 31, Pozieres Memorial. From the *Meath Chronicle*, 21 April

1917, 'Sergt. John Aughey, of Columba Terrace, Kells, was mentioned in despatches for gallant conduct in the field.'

AUGHEY, Owen: Private, Argyll and Sutherland Highlanders, 1st/8th Battalion, S/15602. Baptised: Kells, 22 December 1895. Son of John and Catherine Aughey, *née* Smith. Brother, John, also killed in the war. Occupation: Labourer. Enlisted: 15 December 1915. Enlistment location: Stirling. Age at enlistment: 19. Residence at enlistment: 186 Bury Road, Rochdale, Lancashire. Killed in action, France & Flanders, 16 May 1917. Memorial: II.E.31, Brown's Copse Cemetery, Roeux.

B

BARNARD, William: Private, Northumberland Fusiliers, 1st Battalion, 3469. Born: Summerhill. Son of Thomas and Sarah Barnard. Father's occupation: Bailiff on the Summerhill Estate. Father had served in Northumberland Fusiliers. Enlistment location: Dublin. Served in France from 13 August 1914. Killed in action, Neuve Chapelle, 11 March 1915. Age: 18. Memorial: Panel 8 and 12, Ypres (Menin Gate) Memorial. Agher Churchyard. 'Barnard, W. Private, Northumberland Fus' (Trim Church of Ireland, Roll of Honour).

BARNES, Peter Joseph: Private, Royal Dublin Fusiliers, 2nd Battalion, 19644. Baptised: Carnaross, 20 May 1883. Son of Bryan or Bernard and Annie Barnes, *née* Smyth, Carnaross, Kells. Residence: Kells. Enlistment location: Cardiff. Killed in action, France & Flanders, 8 November 1918. Age: 35. Memorial: In north-east part, Floursies Churchyard.

BARNEWALL, The Hon. Reginald Nicholas Francis Mary: Captain Leinster Regiment, 5th Battalion, attached to 2nd Battalion, Son of Charles Aloysius Barnewall, 18th Baron Trimlestown, Wilmount, Kells. Died of wounds, France & Flanders, 24 March 1918. Age: 20. Memorial: II.E.41, Bronfay Farm Military Cemetery, Bray-Sur-Somme.

BAYLY, Maurice Fitzgerald: Sapper, Canadian Engineers, 1st Battalion, 507701. Born: Moylough, Co. Galway, 19 February 1889. Son of Maurice Spring and Jeanie Theodora Bayly, Lisclogher, Athboy. Occupation: Miner. Enlisted: 17 December 1916. Enlistment location: Crowborough. Height: 6 foot 1½ inches. Complexion: Fair. Eyes: Blue. Hair: Brown. Died of shell shock, France & Flanders, 6 August 1918. Age: 27. Memorial: II.A.21, Ligny-St Flochel British Cemetery, Averdoingt.

BEHAN, Thomas: Private, Cameron Highlanders, 7th Battalion, S/27054. Formerly Lovat Scouts, 5913. Baptised: Trim, 12 July 1892. Son of John and Bridget Behan, *née* O'Toole. Residence: Glasgow. Enlistment location: Glasgow. Killed in action, France & Flanders, 23 August 1918. Age: 25. Memorial: III.A.6, Hersin Communal Cemetery Extension.

BENNETT, James: Private, also listed as Company Sergeant-Major, Leinster Regiment, 3rd Battalion, 5396. Born: Kells. Enlistment location: Birr. Died of wounds, home, 21 November 1917. Awards: CSM, DCM. Memorial: CE. 669, Grangegorman Military Cemetery.

BERGIN, Joseph: Oldcastle. From the *Meath Chronicle*, 3 October 1914, 'Oldcastle Men killed in the War. Deep regret has been occasioned in the Oldcastle district by the news that John Gaughran, Ballinlough; Private Smith, Fennor and Joseph Bergin, Oldcastle have been killed in the war.'

BERRY, Harry Albert: Sergeant, London Regiment (Royal Fusiliers), 1st/2nd Battalion, 230396. Born: Loughcrew, 9 December 1894. Eldest son of James William and Mary Ellen Berry, *née* Coggins, Loughcrew, Oldcastle. Father's occupation: Groom and Domestic Servant. Educated Loughcrew and Skerry's College, Dublin. Occupation: Civil Service Clerk. Residence: Loughcrew. Enlistment location: Westminster, 5 August 1914. Went to Malta, September 1914. Sent to France in January 1915. Wounded at Hooge in July 1915 and on recovery in December served with the Egyptian Expeditionary Force in Egypt and Palestine. Returned to France in May 1916 and was reported as missing after the fighting at Glencorse Wood, 16 August 1917. Killed in action, France & Flanders, 16 August 1917. Age: 23. Awards: Mentioned in Despatches for gallant and distinguished service in the field and was awarded the Military Cross for his assistance to wounded under heavy shell fire, while severely wounded himself. Unmarried. Memorial: Panel 52, Ypres (Menin Gate) Memorial. From the *Meath Chronicle*, 22 September 1917, 'As a result of the recent "big push" on the Western Front, many Oldcastle names occur in the casualty lists, including Mr. Webb, Hilltown, Mr. Berry, Loughcrew, also a man named Tuite, who belonged to the Australian contingent.' From the First World War Memorial, St Kieran's church, Loughcrew, 'Sergt Harry Berry – M.M.R.F.'

Harry Berry on his last home leave. (Courtesy Meath County Library)

BIRD, Michael: Private, Royal Dublin Fusiliers, 6th Battalion, 23269. Born: Trim. Baptised: Trim, 29 January 1880. Son of Michael and Elizabeth Bird, *née* Cook, Scarlett Street, Trim. Father's occupation: General Labourer. Michael Bird married Julia Curtis, both of Church Street, on 2 July 1899 at Trim. Children: Michael, John, James, Kathleen, Patrick and Elizabeth Mary. Residence: Haggard Street. Occupation: Bread Van Driver. Enlistment location: Dublin. Died: Balkans, 8 September 1917. Age: 37. Memorial: 1178, Salonika (Lembet Road) Military Cemetery. From Trim Church of Ireland, Roll of Honour, 'Bird, M. Private, Royal Dublin Fusiliers.'

BLAKE, John: Lance-Corporal, Leinster Regiment, 1st Battalion, 5544. Born: Navan, about 1885. Son of John and Margaret Blake, Flower Hill, Navan. Husband of Rose Anne Blake, *née* McGillick, Cannon Row, Navan. Employed as billiard marker before becoming employee of Meath County Council for sixteen years. Enlistment location: Drogheda. Died of sickness, 17 October 1918. Age 33. Memorial: S.3., Ramleh War Cemetery, Israel.

BLIGH, Frederick Arthur: Major, Royal Field Artillery, B Battery. 154th Brigade. Formerly with the RHA. Rejoined on the outbreak of war after twenty-one years of retirement. Born: 3 July 1861, only son of Major Frederick Cherburgh Bligh and Emily Matilda East, Brittas, Nobber. Born: Farnham, Surrey, 3 July 1861. Educated: Cheltenham College and the Royal Military Academy, Woolwich. Gazetted Lieutenant R.A. 1881, and later Captain. Served in Chestnut Troop RHA and retired in 1895 after twelve years' service. Succeeded his father in the Brittas estates 30 November 1901. Justice of the Peace. High Sheriff 1904. Married Mary Wentworth-Forbes at Rochester Cathedral, 22 June 1898. Left a daughter, Gwendolen Mary, born 19 January 1905. Volunteered his services on the outbreak of the European War and in June 1915 was called upon to train B Battery, 154th Brigade, RFA 'in connection with the Ulster Division' at Okehampton. Though there was hardly a trained man among them when it started they were ready for the front at the end of October 1915. On the last day of training he fell ill with appendicitis and died soon afterwards. Died in hospital, on active service, 15 November 1915. His wife died 4 November 1928 and is buried in the same grave. Memorial: New. 17.56, Headley (All Saints') Churchyard. From the *Meath Chronicle*, 20 November 1915:

Death of Major F.A. Bligh R.F.A. The news of the death of Major Frederick Arthur Bligh R.F.A. of Brittas, Nobber, which took place at Oakhampton on Monday after an operation for appendicitis contracted while on duty, was heard with much regret by the people of Nobber and neighbourhood. He belonged formerly to the Chestnut Troop R.H.A. but had retired for some years. When the war broke out he offered his services to his old corps and trained a battery of field artillery in connection with the Ulster Division. A military funeral took place at Headley, Hants, on Thursday.

BLIGH, John: Private, Northumberland Fusiliers, 26th Tyneside Irish Battalion, 26/799. Secondary Regiment: Labour Corps, transfered to 396904, 783rd Area Employment Company. Born: Dublin, 1878. Brother of Patrick Bligh, Kilmer, Ballivor. Enlistment location: East Street, South Shields. Enlisted 10 December 1914, aged 36. Occupation: Labourer. Height: 5 foot 8 inches. Died as a result of a fractured skull, First Northern General Hospital, 17 March 1918. Memorial: Q.U.372, Newcastle upon Tyne (St Andrew's and Jesmond) Cemetery.

BLIGH, Thomas: Private, Coldstream Guards, 2nd Battalion, 2829. Baptised: Ballivor, 25 May 1878. Son of Andrew and Anne Bligh, née Kearney, Ballivor. Residence: Ballivor. Enlistment location: Dublin. Killed in action, France & Flanders, 27 August 1918. Age: 40. Memorial: III.A.22, Croisilles British Cemetery.

BOHAN, Robert Joseph: Private, Royal Army Service Corps, T1/4242. Born: Kentstown. Baptised: Beauparc, 1 April 1891. Son of John and Bridget Bohan, née Keating, Flemingstown. Brother, William, also killed in the war. Father's occupation: Agricultural Labourer. Occupation: Labourer. Enlisted 13 August 1914. Enlistment location: Kilcaldy. Eyes: Blue. Hair: Dark Brown. Served in France from 29 May 1915. Discharge unfit due to diabetes, 21 March 1918. Died 13 April 1919. Age: 27. Memorial: Danestown Graveyard.

BOHAN, William: Private, Cheshire Regiment, 13th Battalion, W/925. Born: Kentstown. Baptised: Beauparc, 27 February 1885. Son of John and Bridget Bohan, née Keating, Horsestown. Brother, Robert, also killed in the war. Father's occupation: Agricultural Labourer. Occupation: Agricultural Labourer. Enlistment location: Port Sunlight. Died of wounds, France & Flanders, 19 January 1918. Age: 33. Memorial: X.D.5, Grevillers British Cemetery.

BOND, Alfred: Lance-Corporal, Leinster Regiment, 2nd Battalion, 5364. Baptised: Kells, 24 May 1898. Son of George and Anne Bond, née Dolan. Residence: Dublin. Enlistment location: Dublin. Killed in action, France & Flanders, 4 September 1918. Memorial: V.C.4, Wulverghem-Lindenhoek Road Military Cemetery.

BOURKE: *see* **LEGGE-BOURKE.**

BOYLAN, Joseph: Lance-Sergeant, York and Lancaster Regiment, 6th Battalion, 10721. Baptised: Navan, 12 April 1890. Son of Joseph and Anne Boylan, *née* Hanlon, Church View. Residence: Sandymount, Navan. Occupation: Labourer. Enlisted: 22 April 1917. Height: 5 foot 6½ inches. Killed in action, France & Flanders, 9 October 1917. Memorial: Panel 125 to 128, Tyne Cot Memorial. Old Athlumney graveyard.

BRADY, Edward: Driver, Royal Field Artillery. 62837. Born: Kells. Son of Mrs Jane Brady, 26 Richmont Place, Edinburgh, Scotland. Enlistment location: Edinburgh. Died: home, 15 September 1916. Memorial: III. 81, Glasgow (St Kentigern's) Roman Catholic Cemetery.

BRADY, Francis: Private, Connaught Rangers, 2nd Battalion, 8722. Residence: Kells. Enlisted: 6 February 1906. Enlistment location: Kells. Served in India 1906-1912. Discharged to Reserves. Recalled in 1914. Wounded at Mons. Invalided home due to poor health in December 1914. Discharged from Army May 1915. Died of TB, home, 17 August 1915. Age: 31. Memorial: in south-east part of St John's Burial Ground, Kells. St John's Graveyard Kells, '2872 Private F. Brady, Connaught Rangers, Date of Death: 17 August 1915 aged 31'.

BRADY, James: Lance-Sergeant, Irish Guards, 2nd Battalion, 3881. Born: Ratoath. Husband of Mrs James Brady, Santry Demesne, Santry, Co. Dublin. Enlistment location: Dublin. Age at enlistment: 18 years. Occupation at enlistment: Farm Labourer. Died at sea, 10 October 1918. Memorial: Hollybrook Memorial, Southampton.

BRADY, John: Rifleman, Royal Irish Rifles, 1st Battalion, 9618. Born: Dunderry. Residence: Nobber. Enlistment location: Dublin. Killed in action, France & Flanders, 23 October 1916. Memorial: Pier and Face 15A and 15B, Thiepval Memorial.

BRENNAN, James John: Lance-Corporal, North Staffordshire Regiment, 7th Battalion, 10469. Born: Dundalk. Son of Mrs Margaret Brennan, Blackrock, Dundalk, Co. Louth. Residence: Julianstown. Enlistment location: Leeks, Staffordshire. Served in Balkans from 2 July 1915. Died of wounds, Gallipoli, 14 August 1915. Age: 20. Memorial: Panel 170 and 171, Helles Memorial.

BRENNAN, Patrick: Private, Household Cavalry and Cavalry of the Line, including Yeomanry and Imperial Camel Corps, (Prince of Wales' Own Royal) Hussars, 10th Battalion, 73697. Formerly South Irish

Horse. Baptised Navan, 1 August 1888. Son of Patrick and Mary A. Brennan, *née* Gough, High Park, Athlumney, Navan. Father's occupation: Groom. Occupation: General Labourer. Residence: Navan. Enlistment location: Dublin. Killed in action, France & Flanders, 9 October 1918. Memorial: II.A.13, Honnechy British Cemetery.

BRIEN, John: Private, Irish Guards, 2nd Battalion, 7028. Born: Kingscourt, Co. Cavan. Son of Jane Mary Brien, The Deans, Duleek. Enlistment location: Drogheda, Co. Louth. Died of wounds, France & Flanders, 8 September 1917. Age: 30. Memorial: I.H.50, Bleuet Farm Cemetery. Drogheda War Memorial.

BRIEN, William Thomas: Private, Royal Irish Regiment, A Company, 5th Battalion, 3428. Born: Randalstown, Navan. Son of William Thomas and Sarah Sophia Brien, Ardkeen, Waterford. Residence: Portlaw, Co. Waterford. Enlistment location: Longford. Killed in action, Gallipoli, 16 August 1915. Memorial: Panel 55, Helles Memorial.

BRODIGAN, Francis John: Captain, Gloucestershire Regiment, 1st Battalion. Born: Portsmouth. Son of Col. Francis Brodigan (28th Gloucestershire Regt.) and Alice Brodigan, Piltown House, Drogheda, Co. Meath. Occupation:

2nd Meath Militia. Killed in action at Festubert, France, 9 May 1915. Age: 31. Memorial: Panel 17, Le Touret Memorial. Drogheda War Memorial. From Julianstown church, stained-glass window, 'Francis John Brodigan, Captain, Gloucestershire Regiment, killed in action at Festubert 9 May 1915.' From the *Drogheda Independent*, 15 May 1915:

Captain Francis J. Brodigan of the 1st Battalion, Gloucestershire Regiment, was killed in action on the 9th inst. He was 31 years of age, and until recently was detained at home in training the New Army. His father, the late Colonel Francis Brodigan, of Piltown House, Drogheda, died in the year 1910. He had been an officer who earned great distinction during the Crimean War, where he fought in the same regiment as that to which his son afterwards belonged.

BROGAN, William Bernard: Acting Corporal, Royal Dublin Fusiliers, 10th Battalion, 26384. Baptised: Trim, 21 August 1895. Son of Michael and Bridget Brogan, *née* Blake, Philistown, Trim. Residence: Trim. Died of wounds, France & Flanders, 22 November 1916. Age: 21. Memorial: VII.D.203, Boulogne Eastern Cemetery. From Trim Church of Ireland, Roll of Honour, 'Brogan, W. Private, Royal Dublin Fusiliers'. From the *Meath Chronicle*, 18 March 1916,

'Recruits from Trim and District. Wm. J. Brogan, Phylistown, Trim, entered the Dublin Fusiliers.' From the *Meath Chronicle,* 2 December 1916:

> Deep regret has been evoked in Trim by the tidings of the death of Private Wm. Brogan, (nephew of Rev. J. Brogan P.P., Moynalty) who succumbed on 22nd Nov., at Boulogne to wounds received in action. Solemn Office and High Mass for the eternal repose of his soul were celebrated in St Patrick's Church, Trim last Monday.

BRUTON, Charles: Private, Irish Guards, 1st Battalion, 7859. Baptised: Beauparc, 6 October 1890. Son of Michael and Catherine Bruton, *née* Brien, Drumree, Dunshaughlin. The family also lived at Sarney, Dunboyne, Graigs, Navan, Batterstown, Powderlough and Kilmur. Father's occupation, Farm Labourer, Shepherd. Occupation: Assistant Shepherd. Enlistment location: Dublin. Died of wounds, France & Flanders, 22 September 1916. Age: 24. Memorial: B.20.69, St Sever Cemetery, Rouen.

BYRNE, George: Private, Irish Guards, 1st Battalion, 4108. Born: Donore, 31 March 1891. Son of George and Margaret Byrne, *née* Reilly, Staleen. Enlistment location: Drogheda. Member of Drogheda Division. Killed in action, Mons, France, 8 November 1914. Memorial: Special Memorial 13, Ypres Town Cemetery Extension. Drogheda War Memorial.

C

CAHILL, James: Shoeing Smith, Army Service Corps, TS/7267. Husband of Sarah Cahill, 22 St Patrick's Terrace, Navan. Three children in 1911 census. Occupation: Blacksmith. Died 27 October 1917. Age: 52. Memorial: Donaghmore Graveyard.

CAHILL, Stanislaus: Served as Matthews. Private, Connaught Rangers, 6th Battalion, 5160. Born: Navan. Son of John and Ellen Cahill, *née* Matthews, Barrack Street, Navan. Residence: Navan. Occupation: Butcher. Enlistment location: Drogheda. Served in the Balkans. Died of wounds, France & Flanders, 6 March 1916. Age: 27. Memorial: V.A.74, Bethune Town Cemetery. From the *Meath Chronicle*, 18 March 1916, 'Intelligence reached Navan during the week of the death in action of Privates Stanislaus Cahill and J. O'Connor, of Navan. Cahill was in the Leinster Regiment and transferred to the Connaught Rangers, and was a native of Navan.'

CAIRNES, William Jameson: Captain, Royal Flying Corps, 74th Squadron, Royal Air Force. Second Lieutenant, 5th Battalion, Leinster Regiment. Born: 7 June 1898. Son of William Plunket and Alice Jane Cairnes, *née* Algar, Stameen, Drogheda, Co. Meath. Father's occupation: Governor of the Bank of Ireland, Chairman Great Northern Railway and Chairman Cairnes (Brewers) Ltd. His brother, Tom Algar Elliott Cairnes, also served in the Royal Flying Corps and another brother, Francis Herbert, served with the Inniskilling Fusiliers, both survived the war. Educated at Rugby and Cambridge. Serving in 5th Leinster Regiment in September 1914. Joined the Royal Flying Corps in Egypt and became a Flying Officer on 6 November 1916. He was promoted to Captain on 20 December 1916. After scoring four victories with 19 Squadron, Cairnes was appointed Flight Commander on 1 February 1918. In the spring of 1918, he scored two more victories with 74 Squadron before he was killed in action. Killed in air combat, over Estaires, France, 6 June 1918. Memorial: Arras Flying Service Memorial, Pas de Calais. Drogheda War Memorial. In St Mary's Church of Ireland church, Drogheda, 'In loving memory of William Jameson Cairnes, Capt. Royal Air Force & Leinster Regiment. Killed in air fight over Estaires on June 1st 1918 in his 22nd year. Much loved youngest son of William & Alice Cairnes.'

CALLAGHAN, John: Wireless Operator, Mercantile Marine, SS

Newminster Abbey, Newcastle upon Tyne. Baptised: Castletown Kilpatrick, 27 September 1892. Son of James and Anne Callaghan, *née* Carpenter, Knightstown, Navan. Father's occupation: Farmer. Died in hospital at Perpignan, as a result of an attack by enemy submarine in the Mediterranean, 11 March 1918. Age: 25. Memorial: Tower Hill Memorial.

CALLAGHAN, Michael: Private, Leinster Regiment, 2nd Battalion, 4772. Baptised Oristown, 29 September 1882. Son of Michael and Anne Callaghan, *née* Horan, Oristown, Kells. Father's occupation: Agricultural Labourer. Enlistment location: Drogheda. Died, France & Flanders, 21 March 1918. Memorial: Sp. Mem. 6, Tinourt New British Cemetery.

CALLAN, Leo: Served as Smith. Fireman, Mercantile Marine, SS *Norwegian*, Liverpool. Son of Patrick Callan, Breslanstown, Drumconrath. Killed as a result of an attack by an enemy submarine or mine, 13 March 1917. Age: 28. Memorial: Tower Hill Memorial, London.

CAMPBELL, Hugh: Private, Seaforth Highlanders, 7th Battalion, S/27866. Son of Hugh and Margaret Campbell, Beauport, Drogheda. Father's occupation: Land Steward. Died of wounds, received in action, France & Flanders, 27 October 1918. Age: 21. Memorial: IV.I.21, Duhallow

A.D.S. Cemetery, Ieper. Drogheda War Memorial.

CAMPBELL, James: Private, Irish Guards, 1st Battalion, 4121. Born: Sheephouse, Drogheda, 25 July 1890. Son of Michael and Jane Campbell, *née* Kelly, Tubberfinn, Donore. Father's occupation: Labourer. Educated at Donore National School. Enlisted 20 May 1912. Enlistment location: Drogheda. Killed in action, Givenchy, France, 11 March 1915. Not married. Memorial: I.D.21, Guards Cemetery, Windy Corner, Guinchy. Drogheda War Memorial.

CAREY, Edward: Lance-Corporal. Irish Guards, 1st Battalion, 3490. Baptised: Rathkenny, 27 July 1888. Son of Nicholas and Elizabeth Carey, *née* Sherlock, Ladyrath, Rathkenny. Father's occupation: Farmer. Enlistment location: Dublin. Killed in action, France & Flanders, 18 May 1915. Memorial: IV.K.40, Guards Cemetery, Windy Corner, Guinchy. Drogheda War Memorial. From the *Drogheda Independent*, 5 June 1915:

Carey – Killed in action in France, May 18th 1915, Lance-Corporal Edward Carey, 1st Battalion No 1 Company Irish Guards, aged 26, third eldest son of the late Nicholas Carey, Ladyrath, Rathkinnay, Co. Meath. Deeply regretted by his fond mother and brothers and a large circle of friends. Sacred Heart of Jesus have mercy on his dear soul. Our Lady, Queen of May, pray for him. RIP.

CAROLAN, Laurence: Rifleman, Royal Irish Rifles. 2nd Battalion, 9975. Baptised: Slane, 15 August 1890. Son of Patrick and Mary Carolan, *née* McGeough, Dowth. Residence: Swords, Co. Dublin. Enlistment location: Drogheda. Killed in action, France & Flanders, 27 October 1914. Memorial: Panels 42 and 43, Le Touret Memorial, Pas-de-Calais. Drogheda War Memorial.

CAROLAN, Terence: Lance-Corporal, Irish Guards, 2nd Battalion, 5531. Born: Barley Hill, Ardagh, Co. Meath. Baptised: Drumconrath, 24 February 1894. Son of James and Jane Carolan, *née* MacIneany, Barley Hill, Kingscourt, Co. Meath. Father's occupation: Agricultural Labourer. Enlistment location: Dundalk, Co. Louth. Killed in action, France & Flanders, 31 July 1917. Age: 20. Memorial: Panel 11, Ypres (Menin Gate) Memorial.

CARR, John: Private, Irish Guards, 1st Battalion, 3332. Born: Ashbourne. Baptised: Curraha, 7 January 1889. Son of Lawrence and Kate Carr, *née* Veldon, Kilbrew, Curraha. Mother's occupation: Charwoman. Enlistment location: Dublin. Killed in action, France & Flanders, 6 November 1914.

Age: 26. Memorial: Panel 11, Ypres (Menin Gate) Memorial.

CARR, Patrick: Private, Irish Guards, 1st Battalion, 3848. Born: Stamullin. Residence: Mullingar, Co. Westmeath. Enlistment location: Wigan, Lancashire. Killed in action, France & Flanders, 6 November 1914. Memorial: Panel 11, Ypres (Menin Gate) Memorial. Drogheda War Memorial.

CARROLL, Christopher: Private, Royal Dublin Fusiliers, 8th Battalion, 23218. Baptised: Trim, 6 May 1893. Son of Christopher and Mary Carroll, *née* Weldon, The Green, Newhaggard Road, Trim. Mother's occupation: Domestic Servant. Killed in action, France & Flanders, 29 April 1916. Age: 23. Memorial: Panel 127 to 129, Loos Memorial. From Trim Church of Ireland, Roll of Honour, 'Carroll, C. Private, Royal Dublin Fusiliers.' From the *Meath Chronicle*, 5 June 1915:

Trim Man's War Experience Private Carroll, Trim of the King's Liverpool Regiment, who was wounded by a bullet in the left leg in Flanders and who is now in Ipswich Hospital, states in a letter to his mother: 'Most of my mates have been shot dead but the Germans got it worse than we did. It was awful to see some poor fellows. I myself had to crawl for nearly a mile on my stomach to get safe. We chased the Germans back three miles and captured their trenches. It is terrible to see what the Germans are doing here: blowing down the large Catholic Churches, leaving them in ruins.

From the *Meath Chronicle*, 15 June 1915:

Meath Soldiers Wounded
Mrs Mary Carroll, Trim, has also been notified that her son, Private Carroll, King's Liverpool Regiment, is at present at Ipswich recovering from a wound received while charging the German trenches.

CARROLL, Frederick Stanley: Second Lieutenant, Royal Inniskilling Fusiliers, 7th Battalion. Baptised: Kells, 28 November 1895. Son of James and Mary Carroll, *née* Forsythe. Father's occupation: Auctioneer. Educated: St Patrick's Cathedral School, Dublin and Kells. Residence: Newmarket Street, Kells. Occupation: Clerk in the Hibernian Bank, Head Office and Drogheda. Joined the 7th Leinster Cadet Corps, February 1915. Gazetted Second Lieutenant August 1916 to 7th Royal Inniskilling Fusiliers. Went to France with his Battalion, in early 1916, was gassed in April and invalided home to hospital for one month. Afterwards he was posted to the Reserve Battalion, of the regiment, returned to France to the 1st Battalion, in October 1916. Killed in action, beyond Guillemont, France, while endeavouring to relieve some men who were isolated, 21 November 1916. A shell fell beside him killing him instantly along with an orderly who was with him. He was buried that night. Killed in action, France & Flanders, 21 November 1916. Age: 20. Memorial XXVI.G.6, Caterpillar Valley Cemetery, Longueval. Unmarried. His Colonel wrote, 'He was a very gallant officer and we all miss him very much'. His Captain also wrote, 'I never knew a braver man.' From War Memorial, 1914–1918, Kells Church of Ireland, '2nd Lieutenant F.S. Carroll, Royal Inniskilling Fus.' From the *Meath Chronicle*, 13 May 1916, 'Second-Lieutenant Frederick S. Carroll (son of Mr. James Carroll, Newmarket Street, Kells) is in hospital, suffering from the effects of a gas attack.' From the *Meath Chronicle*, 2 December 1916:

Kells Officer Killed in Action
We much regret to state that Lieutenant Frederick S. Carroll, fourth son of Mr. James Carroll, Kells, has been killed in action. The sad news reached his parents by wire last Saturday morning. Beyond stating that the gallant young lieutenant was killed on the 21st November, the telegram gave no details. Mr and Mrs Carroll have received numerous messages of condolence and it should be added that deep sympathy for

them is felt amongst every class in the community. Lieutenant Carroll, who wanted a few days of 21 years, was on the staff of the Hibernian Bank at Drogheda when the war broke out. He had previously been attached to the Head Office in Dublin. Shortly after the commencement of the war he enlisted and was gazetted a lieutenancy in the Inniskilling Fusiliers. Having undergone the usual course of training, he went to the front sometime this year. He had not been long in the field of action when he was "gassed," as a result of which he was rendered unfit for service for some considerable time. Having recuperated he returned to France a few weeks ago. He went away in the highest spirits, little dreaming that his career was so soon to end. By his brother officers and comrades his loss will sincerely deplored. He was of a singularly bright and winning disposition, and as manly and chivalourous as he was gentle, guileless and unassuming.

From the *Meath Chronicle*, 16 December 1916:

Mr. James Carroll, Newmarket Street, Kells has received a telegram from the King and Queen warmly sympathising with him and his relatives on the loss of his son Lieutenant Frederick S.

Carroll recently killed in action. Mr. Carroll has also received the following letter:

2nd December 1916
Dear Mr. Carroll,
I regret very much to tell you that your son Lieut. F.S. Carroll was killed on the 21st of November. He was arranging about a relief. A chance shell killed him instantaneously and fatally wounded an orderly who was with him. We buried him that night near where he was killed just behind our front line trenches. He was a promising and gallant officer and we all miss him very much.
Yours truly,
Hardress Llyod
Lt. Col. 1st Iniskillings

CARROLL, J.: Private, Leinster Regiment. 3474. Secondary Regiment: Labour Corps. 487906. Died: 6 May 1919. Memorial: Plot A. 710, Navan New Cemetery.

CARROLL, Matthew: Private, Leinster Regiment, 2nd Battalion, 8385. Baptised: Navan, 30 August 1886. Son of Mathew and Kate Carroll, *née* Briody, Academy Street, Navan. Father's occupation: General Labourer. Residence: Alexander Reid, Athlumney. Enlistment location: Navan. Killed in action, France & Flanders, 20 October 1914. Age: 28. Memorial: Panel 10, Ploegstreet Memorial.

CASEY, Christopher: Private, Leinster Regiment, 1st Battalion, 10239. Born: Navan. Enlistment location: Birr. Killed in action, Salonica, 30 May 1917. Memorial: VII.B.1, Struma Military Cemetery.

CASSERLY, Edward: Private, Royal Dublin Fusiliers, 8th Battalion, 13414. Baptised: Bohermeen, 4 January 1889. Son of David and Catherine Casserly, *née* Brady, Jamestown, Bohermeen. Father's occupation: Farmer. Died 27 April 1916. Age: 24. Memorial: Panel 127 to 129, Loos Memorial.

CASSIDY, Edward: Private, Royal Dublin Fusiliers, 8th Battalion, 13414. Baptised: Bohermeen, 30 January 1868. Son of Thomas and Mary Cassidy, *née* Harte. Residence: Jamestown, Co. Meath. Enlistment location: Coatsbridge. Killed in action, France & Flanders, 27 April 1916. From the *Meath Chronicle*, 27 May 1915, 'A heavy toll of killed, wounded and missing has resulted from the recent fighting in Flanders. The casualty list contains the following names – … Pte. E. Cassidy, Navan, Dublin Fusiliers …'

CASSIDY, James Joseph: Private, Royal Irish Fusiliers, 1st Battalion, 20636. Born: Ross, Co. Meath. Son of James Cassidy, Glasslough Street, Monaghan. Residence: Monaghan. Died of wounds, France & Flanders, 10 September 1918. Age: 21. Memorial: VII.A.8, Arneke British Cemetery.

CASSIDY, Joseph: Private, King's Shropshire Light Infantry, 8th Battalion, 13742. Born: Navan. Residence: Navan. Enlistment location: Wrexham. Killed in action, Salonica, 27 November 1916. Age: 49. Memorial: Doiran Memorial.

CASSIDY, Richard: Private, Royal Inniskilling Fusiliers, 5th Battalion, 20076. Baptised: Drumconrath 15 November 1891. Son of Richard and Ellen Cassidy, *née* Keenan, Summerhill. Enlistment location: Clydebank. Killed in action, France & Flanders, 10 October 1918. Memorial: 7, Reumont Churchyard.

CASSIDY, Thomas: Private, Irish Guards, 1st Battalion, 3452. Born: Harristown. Enlistment location: Navan. Died of wounds, France & Flanders, 9 November 1914. Memorial: IV.D.11, Larch Wood (Railway Cutting) Cemetery.

CERUMNEY, James: Private, Royal Dublin Fusiliers, 8th Battalion, 16199. Born: Athboy. Son of James and Annie Cerumney (or Crummey), Martinstown, Athboy. Father's occupation: General Labourer. Residence: Athboy. Enlistment location: Drogheda. Killed in action, France & Flanders, 6 April 1916. Age: 26. Memorial: Panel 127 to 129, Loos Memorial.

CHAMBERS, Edward Chandos Elliott: Second Lieutenant,

Lancashire Fusiliers, A Company, 19th (Service) Battalion, Only son of Richard Edward Elliot Chambers and Edith Frances Chambers. Educated at Marlborough, Paris and Oxford, where he joined the army through the OTC on 15 June 1915. Died 1 July 1916. Age: 20. Memorial: I.A.13, Bouzincourt Communal Cemetery Extension. From the *Meath Chronicle*, 15 July 1916, 'Second-Lt. E. Chandos E. Chambers, Lancs. Fusrs., killed at the age of 20 years, was the only son of Mr and Mrs R.E. Chambers of Fosterstown, Trim.' From *De Ruvigny's Roll of Honour, 1914-1924,* Volume 2:

Chambers, Edward Chandos Elliot, 2nd Lieutenant, 19th Service Battalion, The Lancashire Fusiliers, only son of Richard Edward Elliot Chambers of Fosterstown, Trim, Co. Meath, resident in England and now of Lyme Regis, Co. Dorset by his wife, Edith Frances, 4th and youngest surviving daughter of the late Henry Chandos–Pole-Gell of Hopton Hall, Co. Derby. Born during his parents' temporary residence in South Africa, at Ailwal North, Cape Colony, 4 April 1896. Educated at Mr. Douglas's, Malvern Link, 5th May 1905-28 July 1909, where he was captain of the school and at Marlborough College, 17 September 1909 – 19 December 1913, where in the Modern Sixth he obtained

"Honourable Mention" as second in the senior Modern Scholarship Examination, and won the Dutton French Prize in 1913. He was in the Marlborough O.T.C. for over three years, and in 1913 was one of the "Cock House" (Sandford's) Cricket XI. and Football XV. After studying in Paris, he obtained on 29 May 1914, a First Class Certificate of the Association Phonétique Internationale, and on 23 June 1914, was elected to an Exhibition in French Language and Literature at St John's College, Oxford where his grandfather Edward Elliott Chambers had graduated with Classical Honours in 1834. There he passed all his examinations except the Final Honour School when, having reached the age of nineteen he was, as a cadet from the Oxford O.T.C., gazetted 2nd Lieutenant 19th (Service) Battalion, Lancanshire Fusiliers 15 June 1915, a Battalion, which some of his Oxford friends were then joining. He joined his regiment on 10 July, at Catterick, in Yorkshire, passed through a course at the Mersey School of Instruction at Formby, in Lancashire (12 July-9 August) and from the second week in August was in training with his regiment for over three months at Codford St Mary, on Salisbury Plain. After a week's bombing course he was appointed early in September, Battalion Bombing Officer, but resigned this some two months later, as training the Grenadiers had prevented his going for further bombing courses, and he was commanding No. 4 Platoon of A Coy, before landing at Havre with his regiment on 22 November 1915. He was in the trenches for the first time on 1 December between La Boiselle and Bécourt, near Albert, that being his furthest point south in the firing line, and when in the trenches was always between Aucre and the Somme, and except for a week's leave in May, served continuously in that part of Picardy. In January he was attached for one month to the 1st Dorsets, who from that time, with the 2nd Manchesters, 19th Lancashire Fusiliers, and 15th Highland Light Infantry formed the 14th Brigade of the 32nd Division. On the morning of the great assault, 1 July, his regiment formed part of one of the leading brigades, and advanced to attack through Authuille Wood, going out from it at the north-east in rushes or waves of five men at a time into open rising ground enfiladed by machine-gun fire. Leading the first wave of his men, he was hit by a machine-gun bullet in the forehead, some thirty-five yards out from the edge of the wood and killed instantaneously "whilst gallantly leading his men to the attack of the German trenches," wrote his Colonel. This was about

9.40 a.m. during the first assault on the Leipzic Redoubt, and about three-quarters of a mile south-south west of Thiepval. He was buried on 3 July, in Bouzincourt Cemetery about two and a quarter miles north-west of Albert. "All the many and warm-hearted testimonies of his brother officers bear witness to the bright and lovable qualities which earned for him the affection of all who knew him at Oxford," says the notice of him in "The Oxford Magazine Extra Number," 10 November 1916. The Rev. H.A. James D.D., President of St John's College, Oxford wrote: "It is our loss, too, for your son was a man of much promise intellectually, bore the highest character, and won the esteem and liking both of his contemporaries among the undergraduates and of his tutors and myself." A Senior Officer wrote: "He had been for a long time now in "A" Coy (my old company) and was a very popular officer; his place will be hard to fill; we are all grieved at the great loss the Battalion, has sustained." The Commanding Officer of his company on 1 July, wrote of " your very gallant son" and that he had never lived with anyone "more cheery and good-natured, and one who did his duty so cheerily and thoroughly, and his loss was very much mourned by all the officers and men of the Battalion … He did all that any man could do, and helped a great many by his optimism and unselfishness." Another says: "He was the best friend anybody could wish for, a fine officer, and knew no fear." Of Oxford friends and brother officers one wrote: "He was afraid of nothing and kept everybody's spirits up by his constant cheerfulness, particularly in the trying conditions of the winter, when we were all new to trench work. I have lost a great friend ... and the regiment has lost a splendid officer." Another a graduate some years senior: "I am bound to say what I know of your son's gallant conduct ... I always admired – some sort of envy - his invincible cheerfulness in the trenches, and the matter-of-fact way in which he went out bombing or with a wiring party into No Man's Land. He was a good officer, a brave man and a gentleman ... He never spared himself and I know that he himself did not grudge the supreme sacrifice. Though I know nothing can make good your loss, yet it will be something to know that his example will live always in the minds of his men and brother officers, as it will live also in the minds of all who knew him in his short but fruitful life.

CLARKE, Cornelius: Private, Irish Guards, 1st Battalion, 4581.

Born: Duleek. Enlistment location: Drogheda. Killed in action, France & Flanders, 4 September 1914. Memorial: 28, Guards' Grave, Villers Cotterets Forest, Aisne.

CLARKE, James: *see* **LANE, James.**

CLARKE, Joseph: Private, East Lancashire Regiment, 2nd Battalion, 9381. Born: Ratoath. Residence: Rochdale, Lancashire. Enlistment location: Dublin. Killed in action, France & Flanders, 10 July 1916. Memorial: Pier and Face 6C, Thiepval Memorial.

CLARKE, Lawrence: Corporal, Royal Irish Rifles, 2nd Battalion, 4981. Formerly Hussars, 13229. Born: Stamullin. Son of Patrick and Bridget Clarke, Gormanstown. Husband of Teresa Clarke, 47 St Joseph's Place, Dorset Street, Dublin. Enlistment location: Dublin. Killed in action, France & Flanders, 24 March 1918. Age: 30. Award: Military Medal. Memorial: Panel 74 to 76, Pozieres Memorial.

CLARKE, Michael Joseph: Able Seaman. Royal Navy, HMS *Defence*, 223863. Baptised: Ratoath, 24 October 1886. Son of Michael and Mary Anne Clarke, *née* Smyth, 16 North Street, Rochdale, Lancashire. Killed in action at Battle of Jutland, 31 June 1916. Age: 30. Memorial: 11, Plymouth Naval Memorial.

CLARKE, Patrick: Lance-Corporal, Irish Guards, 1st Battalion, 1813. Born: Dangan, Co. Tipperary. Residence: Trim. Enlistment location: Clonmel, Co. Tipperary. Husband of Bridget Clarke, 10 Castle Street, Trim. Killed in action, France & Flanders, 1 December 1917. Age: 36. Memorial: Panel 2 and 3 Cambrai Memorial, Louverval. From Trim Church of Ireland, Roll of Honour, 'Clarke, P. Sgt, Irish Guards.' From the *Meath Chronicle*, 26 January 1918, 'Lance-Cpl. P. Clarke, Trim and Private T. McCormack, Kells, both of the Irish Guards, have been officially reported as missing.'

CLARKE, Stephen: Revd Chaplain 4th Class, Army Chaplains' Department, Lancashire Fusiliers, attached 9th Battalion, Killed in action, France & Flanders, 4 October 1917. Memorial: Panel 160, Tyne Cot Memorial. From the *Meath Chronicle*, 15 December 1917, 'Solemn Office and Requiem Mass was celebrated last week in Bruskey, Ballintemple R.C. church for the repose of the soul of the late Rev. Captain Stephen Clarke, a native of Tierworker, Co. Meath, who was killed in the war.'

CLARKE, William Byrne: Sergeant, 6th Dragoons (Inniskilling). 2103. Also Household Cavalry and Cavalry of the Line, including Yeomanry and Imperial Camel Corps. Born: Ballycastle, Co. Mayo. Residence: Clonmellon, Co. Westmeath. Enlistment Location: Bombay, India. Killed in action, France & Flanders, 28 June 1916. Age: 33. Memorial: Pier and Face 1A, Thiepval Memorial. From the *Meath Chronicle*, 22 July 1916, 'Wednesday's list of casualties contained the names of W.B. Clarke, Athboy (killed) and …'

CLARKIN, Patrick: Private, Irish Guards, 2nd Battalion, 6719. Baptised: Dunderry, 7 March 1891. Son of Philip and Anne Clarkin, *née* Loughran, Shambo, Robinstown, Navan. Father's occupation: Farmer and Contractor. Husband of Mary Ann Clarkin, Grennan, Oldcastle. Enlistment location: Drogheda. Killed in action, France & Flanders, 30 September 1915. Age: 27. Memorial: Panel 9 and 10, Loos Memorial.

CLINTON, Thomas: Private, Royal Dublin Fusiliers, 2nd Battalion, C Company. 5616. Baptised: Navan, 21 September 1896. Son of Laurence and Catherine Clinton, *née* Kerly, Brewshill, Navan and later of 10 Luke Street, Dublin. Enlistment location: Dublin. Killed in action, France & Flanders, 25 April 1915. Age: 18. Memorial: Panel 44 and 46, Ypres (Menin Gate) Memorial.

CODDINGTON, Hubert John: Captain, Durham Light Infantry, 2nd Battalion. Born: 1877. Residence: Oldbridge. Served in the Boer War 1898-1901. Killed in action at Ypres, France, 7 July 1915. Memorial: I.N.31.,

La Brique Military Cemetery No. 2. Drogheda War Memorial. From Julianstown church, stained-glass window, 'Hubert John Coddington Captain Durham Light Infantry killed in action Ypres 7th July 1915.' From First World War Memorial, St Kieran's Church, Loughcrew, 'Capt. Hubert J. Coddington 2nd D.L.I.'

COLCLOUGH, Michael Joseph: Lance-Corporal, Irish Guards, 2nd Battalion, 6908. Born: Navan, about 1891. Son of James and Margaret Colclough, Kells Road, Navan. Father's occupation: Gatekeeper, Railway. Served in Navan Irish National Volunteers. Enlistment location: Drogheda, Co. Louth. Died of wounds, France & Flanders, 1 October 1915. Age: 24. Memorial: IV.H.4, Etaples Military Cemetery. From the *Meath Chronicle*, 2 October 1915. Colclough was dead the day before the date of issue of the paper:

Navan Soldier's Story
A Navan gentleman has received the following letter from Corpl. Colclough of the Irish Guards, dated "France 9th Sept – I suppose you have been watching a line from me for many a day. I take this opportunity of dropping you a line. I am quite well and rather enjoying this new experience. We find things rough betimes, but you have one consolation – when you are finished duty you are fin-

ished till the next day. We met the 1st Battalion, some time ago. I was speaking to Pat Fox. He is well and you would think it was in the 'Mollies' we were again, we settled down so comfortably for a chat. He is slightly thinner than usual but otherwise seems as good as ever. He wishes to be remembered to you. I also met young McIneeny, who was in the Post Office. I saw him as we passed through the town in which he is stationed. I called him. He was quite surprised to see me. He also looks fit.

This is a fine country for agriculture. All around you as far as you can reach is nothing but crops in their various stages. The people are very hard-working. They begin their days about 5.30 a.m. and finish often about 7 or 8 o'clock that evening. Here and there are patches of clover, in which cattle, mostly milch cows, are tethered out. I have spent a couple of evenings giving the people with whom we are billeted a hand to get in the corn. We have a Catholic chaplain attached to our regiment. He is a fine man and ranks as captain. We have Mass every Sunday and there is every opportunity given to fulfil your other religious duties. Any evening we happen to be in billets we have Rosary and Benediction in the local church. The country around simply teems with religious emblems. At every cross roads you find huge crosses and here and there along the road are small shrines, as well as statues of the Blessed Virgin set in the gable ends of many houses. Pig rearing also seems to be an industry in this part of the country.

John Sherlock has transferred to the 1st Battalion. He is a signaller. We went for a swim one day and one of our fellows got into difficulties and caught hold of a swimmer who happened to be passing and I believe Sherlock brought both in. The river was narrow but very deep: but you would know anyone who learned swimming at the Metal Bridge could never be beaten in a stiff stream. There is a little more noise out here than we used to make when we were shooting at the slopes.

From the *Meath Chronicle*, 4 December 1915, 'Lance Copl. Michael Colclough, aged 24, Navan, 2nd Batt. Irish Guards, has died in France of wounds received in action on October 29th. The deceased was much esteemed in Navan, where the sad news evoked keen regret, and occasioned deep sympathy with members of his family.'

COLEMAN, Thomas: Private, Leinster Regiment, D Company, 2nd Battalion, 9834. Born: Dublin. Residence: Athboy. Son of Mary Coleman, *née* McCormick, Bridge Street, Athboy. Mother's occupation:

District Nurse. Enlistment location: Drogheda. Killed in action, France & Flanders, 20 October 1914. Age: 20. Memorial: Panel 10, Ploegsteert Memorial.

COLGAN, John: Private, Royal Dublin Fusiliers, 8th Battalion, 23559. Baptised: Rathmolyon, 19 June 1888. Son of Patrick and Margaret Colgan, *née* Farrelly, Ballindern, Enfield. Father's occupation: Labourer. Occupation: General Labourer. Enlistment location: Dublin. Killed in action, France & Flanders, 1 April 1916. Age: 27. Memorial: C.5, Bois-Carre Military Cemetery, Haisnes.

COLLINS, George: Private, Guards Machine Gun Regiment, 4th Battalion, 1031. Formerly Irish Guards, 1002. Born: Lucan, Co. Dublin. Enlistment location: Dublin. Husband of Anne Collins, Knockumber, Navan. Died of wounds, France & Flanders, 12 October 1918. Age: 37. Memorial: I.A.1, Carnieres Communal Cemetery Extension.

COLLINS, James: Private, Connaught Rangers, 1st Battalion, 9224. Born: Ballinabrackey, Kinnegad, Co. Meath. Residence: Tipperary. Enlistment location: Mullingar. Collins and the 1st Battalion came from India and landed at Marseilles in September 1914. Collins went back thorough Marseilles in December 1915 when the Connaught Rangers were sent to Mesopotamia. Died on a hospital ship while being invalided/evacuated from Basra to India, most likely a victim of cholera. Died at sea, 10 August 1916. Memorial: Panel 40 and 64, Basra Memorial.

CONLON, Owen: Private, Leinster Regiment, 7th Battalion, 5016. Baptised: Ballivor, 4 January 1890. Son of John and Elizabeth Conlon, née Dempsey, Ballivor. Father's occupation: Agricultural Labourer. Residence: Ballivor. Occupation: Farm Servant. Enlistment location: Trim. Killed in action, France & Flanders, 8 March 1917. Memorial: K.5, Pond Farm Cemetery.

CONLON, Richard: Private, Connaught Rangers, 5th Battalion, 15322. Formerly Leinster Regiment, 4317. Born: Co. Carlow. Nephew of Nicholas Simmons, Addinstown, Co. Westmeath. Brother of Mrs May Branley, Suffolk Street, Kells. Residence: Athboy. Occupation: Farm Servant. Enlistment location: Navan. Killed in action, 8 October 1918. Memorial: A. 22, Serain Communal Extension.

CONLON, Thomas: Private Royal Dublin Fusiliers, 9th Battalion, 23914. Baptised: Duleek, 5 June 1896. Son of Richard and Bridgid Conlon, née McCabe, Larrix Street, Duleek. Father's occupation: Farmer. Residence: Duleek. Enlistment location: Drogheda. Killed in action, France & Flanders, 6 September 1916. Age: 20. Memorial: XIV.E.4, Guillemont Road Cemetery. Drogheda War Memorial.

CONNOLLY, James: Lance-Sergeant, Irish Guards, 2nd Battalion, 6452. Born: Moate, Co. Meath. Killed in action, France & Flanders, 23 March 1918. Memorial: Bay 1, Arras Memorial.

CONNOLLY, Laurence: Private, Royal Dublin Fusiliers, 9th Battalion, 22151. Baptised: Navan, 13 October 1882. Parents: Michael and Kate Connolly, née Kennedy, Chapel Lane, Navan. Father's occupation: Sheep Dealer. Residence: Navan. In 1911 boarding in Poolboy Street with Patrick Ratty. Occupation: General Labourer. Enlistment location: Dublin. Killed in action, France & Flanders, 23 August 1916. Age: 33. Memorial: Panel 127 to 129, Loos Memorial. From the *Meath Chronicle*, 28 October 1916, 'Pte. L. Connolly of Navan is believed to be missing.'

CONNOLLY, Patrick: Private, Lancashire Fusiliers, 1st Battalion, 4317. Baptised: Athboy, 11 July 1890. Son of Joseph and Anne Connolly, née McGovern, The Green, Athboy. Father's occupation: Horse Trainer. Residence: St Helen's, Lancashire. Enlistment location: Liverpool. Killed in action, Gallipoli, 14 June 1915. Memorial: XI.E.17, Twelve Tree Copse Cemetery.

CONNOR, Christopher: Gunner, Royal Garrison Artillery, 122nd Heavy Battery, 41999. Born: Kilmore. Residence: Kilmore. Enlistment location: Dublin. Killed in action, France & Flanders, 30 September 1917. Memorial: XII.G.21, Vlamertinghe New Military Cemetery.

CONNOR, James: Private, Royal Fusiliers City of London Regiment, 2nd/2nd London, 67495. Formerly ASC S/4/217252. Born: Trim. Enlistment location: Trim. Killed in action, 26 October 1917. Memorial: Panel 28 to 30 and 162 to 162A and 163A, Tyne Cot Memorial. Possibly **CONNER, Jas**: Private, Leinster Regiment (Trim Church of Ireland, Roll of Honour)

CONNOR, Patrick: Private, Royal Dublin Fusiliers, 10th Battalion, 6897. Born: Skryne. Enlistment location: Naas, Co. Kildare. Died: France & Flanders, 19 March 1918. Memorial: 76.K.10, Grimsby (Scartho Road) Cemetery.

CONNORS, Joseph: Private, Connaught Rangers, 1st Battalion, 8716. Born: Trim. Residence: Trim. Enlistment location: Navan. Killed in action, France & Flanders, 23 November 1914. Possibly: **CONNER, Jos**. Private, Leinster Regiment (Trim Church of Ireland, Roll of Honour)

CONNORTON, W.: Trimmer, Mercantile Marine, SS *Vedamore* Liverpool. Born in Co. Meath. Drowned as result of an attack by an enemy submarine or a mine, 7 February 1917. Age: 32. Memorial: Tower Hill Memorial, London.

CONYNGHAM, Victor George Henry Francis: Lieutenant, Royal Irish Regiment, 7th South Irish Horse Battalion, 5th Marquess of Conyngham. Eldest son of Henry Francis, 4th Marquess Conyngham, and his wife Frances Elizabeth Sarah Eveleigh De Moleyns, Slane Castle. Died 9 November 1918. Age: 35. He was baptised on 17 March 1883 at Patrixbourne, Kent. He was styled as 'Earl of Mount Charles' between 1883 and 1897. He was educated between 1896 and 1899 at Eton College. He succeeded to the title of '5th Marquess of Conyngham' on 28 August 1897. He gained the rank of Lieutenant in the service of the 3rd Battalion, Wiltshire Regiment. He fought in the Boer War in 1902. Memorial: Slane, St Patrick's Church of Ireland Churchyard in north-west corner. Inscription reads, 'In loving memory of Victor George Henry Francis, 7th Baron, 5th Marquess Conyngham. Lieutenant, South Irish Horse. Born in London, January 1883. Died at Dringthorpe, York, November 1918.' Victor George Henry Francis Conyngham, 5th Marquess Conyngham was born on 30 January 1883 at Charles Street, Berkeley Square, London. His brother, Frederick William

Burton Conyngham, 6th Marquess Conyngham, who also fought in the war, succeeded him as Marquess.

COOGAN, Michael: Private, Leinster Regiment, 5th Battalion, 5716. Born: Donore, 23 October 1900. Son of Laurence and Mary Coogan, *née* Craven, Oldbridge and later of 98 Scarlet Street, Drogheda, Co. Louth. Father's occupation: Shepherd. Residence: Drogheda. Enlistment location: Drogheda. Died at home. 22 February 1918. Memorial: In south corner of Haddington Roman Catholic Graveyard, East Lothian. Drogheda War Memorial.

COWLEY, Joseph: Private, Leinster Regiment, 1st Battalion, 4901. Born: Navan, about 1876. Son of John Cowley, 1 Rafferty's Lane, Navan. Father's occupation: General Labourer. Occupation: General Labourer. Enlistment location: Navan. Died of wounds, France & Flanders, 19 March 1915. Memorial: J.41, Bailleul Communal Cemetery (Nord).

COX, Patrick: Private, King's Liverpool Regiment, 2/8th Battalion, 308700. Baptised: Trim, 5 May 1896. Son of Peter and Elizabeth Cox, *née* Wiley. Killed in action, France & Flanders, 31 October 1917. Memorial: III.A.6, Cement House Cemetery.

COYLE, Michael: Private, Irish Guards, 1st Battalion, 9402. Born: Cortown. Baptised: Girley, 4 December 1893. Son of John and Mary Coyle, *née* Healow, Balrathboyne, Cortown, Kells. Father's occupation: Agricultural Labourer. Occupation: Agricultural Labourer. Enlistment location: Drogheda. Died of wounds, France & Flanders, 28 September 1916. Age: 23. Memorial: I.D.7, Abbeville Communal Cemetery Extension.

COYLE, Patrick: Private, Royal Marine Light Infantry, 2nd Royal Marine Battalion. Born: Donore, 2 February 1896. Occupation: Indoor Servant. Enlisted: 7 October 1913. Enlistment location: Dublin. Served at Plymouth, Mudros and Salonika bases. Joined 2nd Royal Marines 21 August 1916 until he was wounded 28 October 1916. Invalided back to Britain on 6 November 1916. Died from Addisons disease at 4.32 p.m. on 3 December 1916, on RN Hospital Haslar. Next of kin: Friend, Mrs K. Kelly, Joint School, Co. Meath. Memorial: B.16.1, Haslar Royal Naval Cemetery.

CREGAN, Patrick Joseph: Private, Leinster Regiment, 6th Battalion, 151. Son of Patrick and Ellen Cregan, Infirmary Hill and later of Circular Road, Navan. Father's occupation: General Labourer. Residence: Navan. Died at sea on the Hospital Ship

Grantully Castle, 27 October 1915. Age: 19. Memorial: 1591, Salonika (Lembet Road) Military Cemetery. Drogheda War Memorial.

CRINION, Michael: Driver, Royal Field Artillery, 2nd Division Ammunition Column. 33988. Born Kentstown, Navan. Baptised Beauparc, 5 December 1880. Son of Patrick and Margaret Crinion, *née* Mullen, Carranstown, Duleek. Father's occupation: Farm Servant. Occupation: Labourer. Enlistment location: Drogheda. Enlisted: 1897. Age at enlistment: 18 years. Also served in Mesopotamia. Died 4 November 1918. Age: 37. Memorial: S.II.P.15, St Sever Cemetery Extension, Rouen. Drogheda War Memorial.

CRONE, David: Private, Irish Guards, 1st Battalion, 5366. Baptised Dunboyne, 30 September 1893. Son of John and Anne Crone, *née* Coady, Castlefarm. Father's occupation: Caretaker and Stud Groom. Mother's occupation: National School Teacher. Residence: Newtown Park, Leixlip, Co. Kildare. Enlistment location: Dublin. Killed in action, France & Flanders, 12 July 1916. Memorial: I.X.7, La Brique Military Cemetery No. 2.

CRONIN, Gerald George: Private, Somerset Light Infantry, 8th Battalion, 34224. Formerly 968 North Somerset Yeomanry. Baptised: Slane, 8 November 1885. Seventh son of Richard Cronin MD, JP and Flora Mary Cronin, *née* Hutchin, Slane. One of six brothers who served. Residence: Wincanton, Somerset. Enlistment location: Bath. Killed in action, France & Flanders, 4 October 1917. Age: 32. Memorial: Panel 41 to 42 and 163A, Tyne Cot Memorial.

CROSBY, Hugh: Private, King's Liverpool Regiment, 5th Battalion, 307584. Born: Trim. Son of John Crosby, Chapel Street, Tullamore. Residence: Liverpool. Enlistment location: Liverpool. Killed in action, France & Flanders, 8 August 1916. Age: 34. Memorial: Pier and Face 1D, 8B and 8C, Thiepval Memorial.

CRYAN, Patrick: Private, Irish Guards, 2nd Battalion, 2679. Born: Enfield. Residence: Dublin. Served in France from 17 September 1915. Killed in action, France & Flanders, 13 September 1916. Memorial: Pier and Face 7D, Thiepval Memorial.

CULLITON, Edward: Private, Royal Dublin Fusiliers, 8th Battalion, attached 1st Battalion, 25995. Baptised: Drumconrath, 9 February 1897. Son of Edward and Margaret Culliton, *née* Martin, Kellystown, Drumconrath. Father's occupation: Plasterer. Enlistment location: Newcastle Upon Tyne. Killed in action, France & Flanders, 6 September 1916. Age: 18. Memorial: XXV.J.7, Serre Road Cemetery No. 2.

CUNNIFFE, John (Jack): Private, Royal Munster Fusiliers, 2nd/4th Battalion, 18291. Formerly Royal Dublin Fusiliers, 10th Battalion, 25123. Baptised: Athboy, 20 January 1887. Son of Michael and Elizabeth Cunniffe, Clifton Lodge, Athboy and later of Cloughbrack, Ballivor. Father's occupation: (1901) Land Steward, (1911) Farmer. Occupation: Clerk. He had passed two exams in accountancy when he joined the Dubliners in 1914. His brothers, James and Michael, also fought in the war and survived. Enlistment location: Ranelagh, Dublin. He was engaged in the battle of Beaumont Hamel in March 1918. Surviving the battle he was mortally wounded near St Omar and died in St Omar Hospital. Died of wounds, France & Flanders, 24 April 1918. Age: 31. His remains were repatriated to Athboy for burial in the family plot. Memorial: V.A.68, Longuenesse (St Omer) Souvenir Cemetery.

CURTIS, Bernard: Private, Royal Irish Fusiliers, 6th Battalion, 17726. Baptised: Drumconrath, 21 June 1895. Son of William and Elizabeth Curtis, née Flanagan, The Baun, Drumconrath, Ardee, Co. Louth. Father's occupation: General Labourer. Occupation: Agricultural Labourer. Enlistment location: Dublin. Served in the Balkans from 7 August 1915. Killed in action, Gallipoli, 9 August 1915. Age: 20. Memorial: Panel 178 to 180, Helles Memorial.

John Cunniffe. (Courtesy of Janice Matthews)

D

DALY, James: Fireman, Mercantile Marine, SS *Brantingham*, Leith. Baptised: Moynalty, 3 March 1895. Son of William and Annie Daly, *née* Lynch, Leitrim Upper. Father's occupation: Farmer. Occupation: Farmer's son. Presumed drowned, 4 October 1916. Age: 21. Memorial: Tower Hill Memorial, London.

DALY, John: Private, Machine Gun Corps (Infantry), 1st Battalion, 71666. Formerly Leinster Regiment, 5013. Born: Monkstown. Enlistment location: Mullingar, Co. Westmeath. Killed in action, France & Flanders, 21 September or 23 November 1918. Memorial: II.F.15, Temple-le Guerard British Cemetery.

DARBY, John: Private, Leinster Regiment, A Company, 2nd Battalion, 9991. Born: Kinnegad, Co. Meath. Son of James and Kate Darby, Rosan, Kinnegad, Co. Westmeath. Residence: Mullingar, Co. Westmeath. Killed in action, France & Flanders, 20 October 1914. Age: 18. First battle of the 2nd Battalion, took place 18–20 October 1914 at Armentieres. Memorial: Panel 10, Ploegsteert Memorial.

DARBY, Patrick: Private, Royal Irish Fusiliers, 1st Battalion, 24805. Baptised: Johnstown, 22 January 1883. Son of Nicholas and Mary Darby, *née* Finnegan. Occupation: Groom. Residence: Alexander Reid, Athlumney. Served in France from 8 September 1914. Died of wounds, War Hospital, Guise, France, 28 March 1918. Memorial: Allied Section, 1126, Guise (La Desolation) French National Cemetery, Flavigny-le-Petit.

DEASE, Maurice James: Lieutenant, Royal Fusiliers, 4th Battalion, Only son of Edmund F. and Katherine M. Dease, of Levington, Mullingar, Co. Westmeath and Culmullen House, Dunshaughlin. One of the first British officer battle casualties of the war and the first posthumous recipient of the Victoria Cross of the war. Killed in action at Nimy during the Battle of Mons, 23 August 1914. Age: 24. Memorial: V.B.2, St Symphorien Military Cemetery. From the *London Gazette*, 16 November 1914: 'Though two or three times badly wounded he continued to control the fire of his machine guns at Mons on 23rd Aug., until all his men were shot. He died of his wounds.' The Victoria Cross citation records:

On 23rd August 1914 at Mons, Belgium, Nimy Bridge was being defended by a single company of Royal Fusiliers and a machine gun section with Lieutenant Dease in command. The gunfire was intense, and the casualties were heavy, but the Lieutenant went on firing in spite of his wounds, until he was hit for the 5th time and was carried away to a place of safety where he died. A private (S F Godley) of the same Battalion, who had been assisting the Lieutenant while he was still able to operate the guns, took over, and alone he used the gun to such a good effect that he covered the retreat of his comrades.

From *What the Irish Regiments Have Done* by S. Parnell Kerr (1916):

Lieutenant Maurice James Dease, 4th Battalion, Royal Fusiliers. During the action at Nimy, north of Mons, on August 23rd, 1914, the machine guns were protecting the crossing over a canal bridge, and Lieutenant Dease was several times severely wounded, but refused to leave the guns. He remained at his post until all the men of his detachment were either killed or wounded, and the guns put out of action by the enemy's fire. Lieutenant Dease was the first officer to gain the Victoria Cross in the war. He was the only son of Mr. Edmund F. Dease, Culmullen, Drumree, Co. Meath. He was killed in the action at Nimy.

From *De Ruvigny's Roll of Honour, 1914-1924,* volume I:

Dease, Maurice James: V.C. Lieutenant 4th Battalion, Royal Fusiliers, only son of Edmund Fitzlaurence Dease, of Culmullen, Drumree, Co. Meath, J.P. and grandson of James Arthur Dease of Turbotston, J.P. D.L., Vice-Lieutenant of Cavan. Born Gaulstown, Coole, Co. Westmeath 28 September 1889. Educated Frognal Park, Hampstead, Stonyhurst College (1903), Army College, Wimbledon, and Military College, Sandhurst. Gazetted 2nd Lieutenant 27 May 1910, promoted Lieutenant 19 April 1912 and on the outbreak of war proceeded with his regiment to France. On 23 August Lieutenant Dease, who was Machine Gun Officer, was in command of the section placed to protect the crossing of a bridge at Nimy, north of Mons. During the action his position was heavily shelled by the enemy, all his men being either killed or incapacitated; he was several times seriously wounded but refused to leave the guns, remaining near and working them until he fell mortally wounded. For this he was specially mentioned in Field Marshal Sir John French's Despatch of 7 September and was awarded the Victoria Cross, 16 November 1914, the first officer to receive this distinction in the war. The action is thus officially described: Though two or three times wounded, he continued to control the fire of his machine guns at Mons on 23 August until all his men were shot. He died of his wounds." His commanding officer wrote: "Lieutenant Dease was wounded, and man after man of his detachment was hit. He appears to have received a second wound after neglecting a first wound in the leg; taking a little time to recover, he managed to return to the gun and kept it in action. He was then incapacitated by a third wound. Thus his conduct was heroic indeed, and of the greatest service in delaying the crossing of the enemy, which it was our object to effect ... I have brought his conspicuous gallantry to notice.

DEMPSEY, Patrick: Private, Royal Dublin Fusiliers, 9th Battalion, 18131. Born: St Mary's, Meath. Brother of Miss Margaret Dempsey, 2 Eugene Street, off Cork Street, Dublin. Enlistment location: Drogheda. Killed in action, France & Flanders, 9 September 1916. Memorial: Pier and Face 16 C, Thiepval Memorial.

DE STACPOOLE, Robert Andrew: Second Lieutenant, Connaught Rangers, 2nd Battalion, Born: 25 May 1892, Mount Hazel, Woodlawn, Ballymacward, Co. Galway. Fourth son of George, Duke de Stacpoole and Pauline May, *née* McEvoy, Mount Hazel, Woodlawn, Co. Galway and Tobertynan House, Longwood. Educated Downside, Wimbledon College and the Royal Military College, Sandhurst. Gazetted 2nd Lieutenant, Connaught Rangers, 20 September 1911 and promoted Lieutenant 22 August 1914. Served with the Expeditionary Force in France and Flanders and was killed in action at Verneuil, during the Battle of the Aisne, 20 September 1914. Unmarried. Memorial: La Ferte-Sous-Jouarre Memorial. From Trim Church of Ireland, Roll of Honour, 'De Stacpoole, R. Lieutenant, Connaught Rangers.' His elder brother, George Edward Joseph Patrick Stacpoole served as Captain 3rd Battalion, Connaught Rangers during the war and survived. He lived at Tobertynan House. Another elder brother, Edward Hubert Michael Stacpoole, served as a Captain in the Leinster Regiment and survived the war. Another elder brother, Francis Gustave Stacpoole, served in the war as Lieutenant in the Irish Guards and was wounded but survived. A younger brother (see below) was killed in the war.

DE STACPOOLE, Roderick Algernon Anthony: Second Lieutenant, Royal Regiment of Artillery (Royal Horse and Royal Field Artillery), 1st Battery. Born: 11 August 1895, Mount Hazel, Woodlawn, Ballymacward, Co. Galway. Fifth and youngest son of George, Duke de Stacpoole and Pauline May, *née* McEvoy, Mount Hazel, Woodlawn, Co. Galway and Tobertynan House, Longwood. Educated Downside, Wimbledon College, and the Royal Academy, Woolwich. Gazetted Second Lieutenant RFA 11 August 1914 and joined the 1st Battery with which he went to France in November with the 8th Division. Killed in action, Neuve Chapelle, France, 11 March 1915. Unmarried. Awards: Mentioned in dispatches (*London Gazette*, 22 June 1915) for gallant and distinguished service in the field. Memorial: VI.A.10, Pont-Du-Hem Military Cemetery, La Gorgue. From *De Ruvigny's Roll of Honour, 1914-1924*, volume 2:

> One of his officers wrote: If you see Humphries tell him how deeply the whole brigade regret the death of the high-spirited boy de Stacpoole. In years only a child, with the face of a girl, he had the heart of a hero. He was killed carrying a telephone across an open fire-swept field. Having put his men in safety, he took the post of danger himself.

'De Stacpoole, R.A. Second Lieutenant, RFA' (Trim Church of Ireland, Roll of Honour). His elder brother, George Edward Joseph Patrick de Stacpoole served as Captain 3rd Battalion, Connaught Rangers during the war and survived. He lived at Tobertynan House. Another elder brother, Edward Hubert Michael Stacpoole, served as a Captain in the Leinster Regiment and survived the war. Another elder brother, Francis Gustave Stacpoole, served in the war as Lieutenant in the Irish Guards and was wounded but survived. Another elder brother (see above) was killed in the war.

DEVINE, Patrick: Private, Leinster Regiment, 3rd Battalion, 9027. Born: Kells. Enlistment location: Navan. Died: home, 23 May 1915. Age: 24. Memorial: In north-east part of St John's Graveyard Kells where it reads, '9072 Private P. Devine, Leinster Regiment. Date of Death: 23 May 1915 age 24.'

DIGNAM, T.: Private. From the *Meath Chronicle*, 29 July 1916, 'Private T. Dignam of the Leinster Regiment, who belonged to Ballybeg, near Kells, was among the many Irish soldiers who fell in the recent heavy engagements in the Somme region of France.'

DIXON, Michael: Sergeant, Connaught Rangers, 6th Battalion, 4/5405. Born: Longwood. Enlisted as a wartime volunteer but probably had previous military experience. Served in France from December 1915. Died at the Battle of Messines. Kiled in action leading a squad of the Connaught Rangers in an attack on a German pillbox near Wytschaete. Killed in action, France & Flanders,

7 June 1917. Age: 39. Memorial: I.A.9, Wytschaete Military Cemetery.

DODDS, William: Private, Royal Scots, 13th Battalion, 41373. Born: Navan. Son of Alexander and Agnes Dodds. Married 26 April 1912, Selkirk. Husband of Euphemia Dodds, *née* Hume, Burn Cottage, Mill Street, Selkirk. Three children, Euphemia, born 1913; Alexander, born 1914, and James born 1916. Residence: Thorburne Buildings, Dalkeith. Occupation: Insurance Agent. Enlisted: 11 December 1915, aged 28 years 8 months. Height: 5 foot 5½ inches. Embarked for France January 1917. Killed in action, France & Flanders, 23 April 1917. Memorial: I.C.18, Windmill British Cemetery, Monchy-le-Preux.

DOHERTY, Thomas: Private, Royal Dublin Fusiliers, 9th Battalion, 26586. Born: Dunsany. Residence: Clavanstown, Co. Meath. Enlistment location: Dublin. Killed in action, France & Flanders, 3 September 1917. Memorial: I.D.23, Croisilles British Cemetery.

DOLAN, Patrick: *see* **LEDDY, Patrick.**

DOMEGAN, Christopher Patrick: Lieutenant, Royal Air Force and Royal Irish Fusiliers. Born: Dublin. Son of Patrick and Catherine Domegan, both natives of Meath, 29

North King Street, Dublin. Father's occupation: Tram Driver. Drowned in the Irish Sea from RMS *Leinster*, 10 October 1918. Age: 22. Memorial: Ardcath Graveyard.

DONNELLY, John: Private, Royal Dublin Fusiliers, 1st Battalion, 20218. Baptised: Ratoath, 13 November 1894. Son of Richard and Margaret Donnelly, *née* Lynch, Lagore Little, Ratoath. Father's occupation: Farmer. Occupation: Groom. Residence: Ratoath. Enlistment location: Dublin. Killed in action, France & Flanders, 1 July 1917. Age: 22. Memorial: Panel 44 and 46, Ypres (Menin Gate) Memorial.

DONNELLY, Thomas: Private, Leinster Regiment, 2nd Battalion, 4622. Husband of Mrs Margaret Donnelly, Barrack Street, Navan. Enlistment location: Mosney Camp, Drogheda. Died of wounds, 18 July 1915. Memorial Reference: BI.5, Potijze Burial Ground Cemetery.

DONOHOE, Joseph: Private, Royal Army Service Corps. M/272403. Baptised: Navan, 8 August 1898. Son of Christopher and Mary Anne Donohoe, *née* Burke, Cornmarket, Navan. Father's occupation: Labourer. Residence: Clydebank. Enlistment location: Dumbarton. Died, home, 18 June, 1917. Memorial: Warlingham (All Saints') Churchyard, Surrey, England.

DORAN, John J.: Private. Irish Guards, 1st Battalion, 4729. Born: Dunshaughlin. Son of Thomas and Catherine Doran, Drumree, Dunshaughlin. Father's occupation: General Dealer. Occupation: General Labourer. Residence: Sallins, Co. Kildare. Enlistment location: Dublin. Served in France from 21 September 1914. Killed in action, France & Flanders, 1 February 1916. Age: 24. Award: Mentioned in dispatches. Memorial: VI.J.1, Merville Communal Cemetery.

DOREY, John: Private, King's Own Scottish Borderers, 6th Battalion, 25646. Born: Dunshaughlin. Residence: Irvine, Ayr. Enlistment location: Irvine, Ayr. Killed in action, France & Flanders, 3 May 1917. Memorial: Bay 6, Arras Memorial.

DOUGHERTY, Thomas: Private, Royal Dublin Fusiliers, 7th Battalion. B Company, 12419. Born: Dublin. Son of Thomas and Mary Dougherty, Charlesfort, Kells. Enlistment location: Dublin. Served in Balkans from 9 August 1915. Killed in action, Gallipoli, 21 August 1915. Age: 21. Memorial: Panel 190 to 196, Helles Memorial.

DOWNEY, Eugene: Private, King's Liverpool Regiment, 1st/8th Battalion, 307874. Born: Oldcastle. Son of Andrew and Mary Downey, Ardee Street, Collon, Co. Louth. Father's occupation: Agricultural Labourer. Occupation: Agricultural Labourer. Residence: Liverpool. Enlistment location: Seaforth, Lancashire. Killed in action, France & Flanders, 31 July 1917. Age: 22. Memorial: Panel 4 and 6, Ypres (Menin Gate) Memorial.

DRUM, Michael: Private, Leinster Regiment, 2nd Battalion, 265. Baptised: Kells, 30 April 1876. Son of John and Bridget Drum, *née* Barrington, Circular Road /Newrath, Kells. Father's occupation: Labourer. Occupation: Labourer. Residence: Drogheda. Enlistment location: Drogheda. Served in Balkans from 9 July 1915. Wounded in the Dardanelles. Killed in action, France & Flanders, 18 August 1916. Age: 40. Memorial: XXV.E.2/4, Serre Road Cemetery No. 2. From the *Meath Chronicle*, 23 September 1916:

Killed in Action
In the list of those killed in action is, we are sorry to notice, the name of another young Kells man, Cpl. Michael Drum, of the Leinster Regiment. His father, John Drum, a respectable workman, lives at Newrath, Lloyd. Sometime ago he was wounded at the Dardanelles. On recovering he went to France where he met his death. R.I.P.

DRUMGOOLE, John: Private, Leinster Regiment, 2nd Battalion, 8044. Born: Oldcastle. Enlistment location: Navan. Served in France from 8 September 1914. Died of wounds, France & Flanders, 11 November 1914 Memorial: III.A.16, Lille Southern Cemetery.

DUFF: From the *Meath Chronicle*, 7 October 1916, 'Two soldiers from Trim district, named Duff and Nolan, are reported killed in action. This brings the total from Trim and its vicinity who have paid the supreme penalty up to fifteen.'

DUFFY, Bernard: Rifleman, Rifle Brigade, 13th Battalion, S/3416. Baptised Skryne, 8 September 1888. Son of Joseph and Margaret Duffy, *née* Lynch, Colvenstown, Tara. Occupation: Servant. Enlisted: London, 10 September 1914. Age at enlistment: 26 years. Height: 5 foot 7 inches. Complexion: Fresh. Eyes: Blue. Hair: Dark brown. He was wounded in action on 1 April 1916 and spent until 1 August 1916 in hospital due to a shrapnel wound to the abdomen. Killed in action, France & Flanders, 11 April 1917. Age: 28. Memorial: Bay 9, Arras Memorial.

DUFFY, Thomas: Private, Irish Guards, 2nd Battalion, 5965. Born: Navan. Residence: Castletown, Co. Meath. Enlistment location: Liverpool, Lancashire. Killed in action, France & Flanders, 27 November 1917. Memorial: Panel 2 and 3, Cambrai Memorial, Louverval.

DUIGNAN, Bernard: Rifleman, Royal Irish Rifles, 7th Battalion, 4763. Baptised: Navan, 11 January 1893. Son of Patrick and Bridget Duignan, *née* Forsythe, Cannon Row, Navan. Father's occupation: Baker. Baptised: as Bryan and listed in 1910 census as Brien. In 1911 census listed as Bernard: Occupation: General Labourer. Enlistment location: Navan. Served in France from 21 December 1915. Killed in action, France & Flanders, 9 September 1916. Age: 24. Memorial: Pier and Face 15A and 15B, Thiepval Memorial.

DUNNE, Hugh: Private, Royal Dublin Fusiliers, 8th Battalion, 22201. Born: Ardagh, Co. Meath. Baptised: Drumconrath, 5 November 1869. Son of Hugh and Kate Dunne, *née* McEntee, Barley Hill. Residence: Kingscourt, Co. Cavan. Enlistment location: Dundalk. Served in France from 20 December 1915. Killed in action, 29 April 1916. Age: 50. Memorial: Panel 127 to 129, Loos Memorial.

DUNNE, John Joseph: Petty Officer Stoker, Royal Navy, HMS *Nessus*, 293288. Baptised Curraha, 12 April 1875. Son of James and Ellen Dunne, *née* Reilly. Husband of Ellen Maud Dunne, 1 Brooklyn Terrace, Camel's Head, Devonport. Died: 1 June 1916. Age: 43. Memorial: 14 Plymouth Naval Memorial.

DUNNE, Joseph: Private, Leinster Regiment, 5th Battalion, 7381. Born: St James', Dublin. Enlistment location: Dublin. Died: home, 4 July 1917. Memorial: Moorechurch Graveyard.

DUNNE, Patrick: Private, Royal Dublin Fusiliers, 2nd Battalion, 25051. Born: Warrenstown. Baptised: Dunboyne, 15 May 1897. Eldest son of Christopher and Margaret Dunne, *née* Smith, Warrenstown, Dunboyne. Residence: Dunboyne. Enlistment location: Dublin. Killed in action, France & Flanders, 27 May 1917. Age: 20. Memorial: H.58, Kemmel Chateau Military Cemetery.

DUNVILLE, John Spencer: Second Lieutenant, Household Cavalry, 1st Royal Dragoons. Born: Portland Place,

Patrick Dunne. (Courtesy Marie Callaghan)

London, 7 May 1896. Second son of John Dunville, Redburn, Holywood, Co. Down, and Sion, Navan, Co. Meath and his wife, Violet, daughter of Gustavus Lambart of Beauparc, Co. Meath. His father, John Dunville, managed Dunville and Co., whiskey distillers, Belfast and was master of the Meath Hounds, 1911-15. His brother Robert, also served in the First World War and survived. Educated at Eton. Joined the army, initially serving as a Second Lieutenant in the Fifth Reserve Regiment of Cavalry. In April 1915 he applied to join the Royal Flying Corps and was accepted, but his course of instruction in aviation was cancelled a few days before he was due to start. He transferred to the 6th (Inniskilling) Dragoons and served in France from 6 June 1915. There he took part in the Battle of Loos in September 1915, and transferred to the First Royal Dragoons in January 1916. In April he contracted trench fever and was invalided to England. He returned to France in December. Died of wounds, France & Flanders, 25 June 1917. Age: 21. Memorials: A.21, Villers-Faucon Communal Cemetery. A magnificent stained-glass window in the grand entrance hall of Redburn House was one of several memorials dedicated to him. Roll of Honour, St Mary's church, Navan. Memorial stone, Holywood Graveyard. Awards: Victoria Cross. It was awarded, as the official record states:

For most conspicuous bravery near Epehy, France, on 24th and 25th June, 1917. When in charge of a party consisting of scouts and Royal Engineers engaged in the demolition of the enemy's wire, this officer displayed great gallantry and disregard of all personal danger. In order to ensure the absolute success of the work entrusted to him, Second-Lieut. Dunville placed himself between an N.C.O. of the Royal Engineers and the enemy's fire, and thus protected, this N.C.O. was enabled to complete a work of great importance. Second-Lieut. Dunville, although severely wounded, continued to direct his men in the wirecutting and general operations until the raid was successfully completed, thereby setting a magnificent example of courage, determination, and devotion to duty to all ranks under his command. The gallant officer has since succumbed to his wounds.

E

EBBITT, Joseph: Sergeant, Royal Dublin Fusiliers, 2nd Battalion, 15797. Born: Longwood. Enlistment location: Dublin. Served in France from 20 December 1915. Killed in action, France & Flanders, 28 March 1918. Award: Military Medal. Memorial: VIII.G.10, Heath Cemetery, Harbonnieres.

ENGLISHBY, James: Private, Royal Irish Fusiliers, 2nd Battalion, 10151. Baptised: Nobber, 19 September 1880. Son of Thomas and Mary Englishby, *née* Carolan, Possextown, Nobber. Father's occupation: Labourer. Served in France from 19 December 1914. Died of pneumonia, 14 November 1918. Age: 38. Memorial: XIX.F.10, Gaza War Cemetery.

ENNIS, Michael: Sergeant, Royal Irish Fusiliers, 1st Battalion, 15951. Baptised: Trim, 25 August 1880. Son of Patrick and Mary Ennis, *née* Mountain, Brannockstown. Occupation: Agricultural Labourer. Residence: Rathmolyon. Enlistment location: Navan. Killed in action, France & Flanders, 12 October 1916. Memorial: Pier and Face 15A, Thiepval Memorial.

F

FARRELL, Francis: Warrant Officer Class II (Company Sergeant Major) Royal Irish Regiment, 7th Battalion, 25262. Formerly South Irish Horse, 1074. Born: Slane. Son of James and Christina Farrell, Lyons, Hazlehatch, Co. Kildare. Residence: New Ross, Co. Wexford. Enlistment location: Dublin. Killed in action, France & Flanders, 21 March 1918. Age: 23. Memorial: Panels 30 and 31, Pozieres Memorial, Somme. Drogheda War Memorial.

FARRELL, J.: From the *Meath Chronicle*, 22 July 1916, 'The names of J. Farrell (Kells), P. Irwin (do.), and W. Moran (Navan), of the Leinster Regiment appeared in Monday's list of casualties.' Horneck states Joseph Farrell, 6th Leinsters, Kells district, wounded.

FARRELL, James: Private, Royal Irish Fusiliers, 1st Battalion, 9499. Born: Oldcastle. Residence: Tue Brook, Liverpool. Enlistment location: Liverpool. Killed in action, France & Flanders, 25 April 1915. Memorial: Panel 42, Ypres (Menin Gate) Memorial.

FARRELL, Patrick: Private, Connaught Rangers, E Company, 2nd Battalion, 7116. Baptised Kells, 19 January 1883. Son of James and Bridget Farrell, *née* Dempsey, Kells and later of Trim. Residence: Swords, Co. Dublin. Occupation: Labourer. Enlistment location: Dublin. Enlisted: 22 May 1901, aged 18 years 6 months. Height: 5 foot 3¾ inches. Posted to India. He served till November 1908 and then became a reservist. He was mobilized on 7 August 1914 at Galway. Killed in action, France & Flanders, 20 September 1914. Memorial: La Ferte-sous-Jouarre Memorial.

FARRELL, Paul: Private, Leinster Regiment, 1st Battalion, 4101. Baptised: Trim, 21 October 1893. Son of Michael and Mary Farrell, *née* Hughes, Patrick Street and later New Haggard Road, Trim. Father's occupation: Farm Servant. Enlistment location: Drogheda. Served in France from 17 February 1915. Killed in action, France & Flanders, 29 September 1915. Memorial: VII.C.8, Assevilliers New British Cemetery. From Trim Church of Ireland, Roll of Honour, 'Farrell, Paul, Private, Leinster Regiment'.

FARRELL, Philip: Private, Royal Dublin Fusiliers, 9th Battalion, 15615. Born: Dangan. Baptised: Summerhill, 14 March 1886. Son of Louis and Anne Farrell, *née* Elliott. Residence: Doolistown, beside Carey's Cross. Occupation: Farmer. Enlistment location: Navan. Served in France from 19 December 1915. Killed in action, France & Flanders, 16 August 1917. Memorial: Panel 144 to 145, Tyne Cot Memorial. Possibly, Farrell, Phil, Private, Leinster Regiment (Trim Church of Ireland, Roll of Honour).

FARRINGTON, John Joseph: Private, Royal Dublin Fusiliers, 9th Battalion, D Company, 25078. Born: Cloona, Johnstown Bridge, Co. Meath. Son of the Patrick Farrington, Cloona House, Johnstown Bridge, Enfield. Residence: Enfield. Enlistment location: Naas. Killed in action, France & Flanders 12 August 1916. Age: 37. Memorial: I.J.4, Philosophe British Cemetery, Mazingarbe.

FAUGHLIN, Patrick: Private, Leinster Regiment, 3rd Battalion, 2818. Born: 1886, Trim. Son of Thomas and Mary Faughlin, Mill Street, Trim. Father's occupation: General Labourer. Married. Husband of Mary Faughlin née Finnegan, Wellington (Emmet) Street, Trim. Sons, Thomas, born 9 February 1913 and Peter born 14 April 1918. Occupation: Labourer. Served in the Militia. Enlisted: 1 July 1908. Enlistment location: Mosney. Age at enlistment: 22 years. Height: 5 foot 6½ inches. Weight: 133 lbs. Complexion: Fair. Eyes: Blue. Hair: Light Brown. Mobilised August 1914. In September-October 1916 Faughlin was hospitalised at St George's Hospital, Malta for slight malaria.

Drowned on RMS *Leinster* off the Irish coast, 10 October 1918. Age: 31. Memorial: Hollybrook Memorial, Southampton. From Trim Church of Ireland, Roll of Honour, 'Faughlin, P. Private, Leinster Regiment.' His widow married Michael Commons and the couple went on to have eight children. Letter by Mary Faughlin:

The Secty
State for War
War Office
London
14-11-18
Sir,
I wish to bring to under your notice the fact that my husband No. 2818 Pte Patrick Faughlin 3rd Batt Leinster Regiment was home on furlough and left here to return to his Regt. at Portsmouth on the 8 of Oct. last and since that time I have heard nothing about him and as he was always in the habit of writing to me regular I am very anxious about him and as my Separation Allowance has been stopped myself and my children are in a deplorable state and as food stuffs are so dear and scarce and having no money I do not know what to do as he left to return to his Regt. about the time the Leinster was sunk, I fear something must have happened him. I therefore earnestly implore you to have inquiries made about him and let me know the result as soon

as possible so that I may take steps to get my Separation Allowance back or in the case of his death a pension.

I am Sir

Your Obt. Servant

Mary Faughlin

Wellington St.

Trim.

FAY, James: Private, Leinster Regiment, 2nd Battalion, 6032. Born: Johnstown. Son of Mrs Mary Fay, Garlow Cross, Navan. Enlistment location: Navan. Reservist. Joined on mobilisation. Served in France from 8 September 1914. Wounded at Mons. Killed in action: France & Flanders, 12 August 1915. Age 35. Memorial: Panel 44, Ypres (Menin Gate) Memorial. Drogheda War Memorial. From the *Meath Chronicle*, 28 November 1914, 'Meathmen Killed and Wounded. James Fay, of the Leinsters, has been wounded in action in France. He is a native of Garlow Cross.'

FAY, Michael: Stoker, 1st Class, Royal Navy, HMS *Brisk*, 21707. Born: Kentstown. Husband of Elizabeth Fay, 3 Aldbrough Avenue, Dublin. Died 2 October 1917. Memorial: 22 Plymouth Naval Memorial.

FEELEY, William: Private, South Lancashire Regiment, 2nd/5th Battalion, 241939. Born: Stackallen, 22 April 1896. Son of William and Julia Feeley, *née* Maguire, Rushwee, Stackallen. Residence: Stackallen. Father's occupation: Agricultural Labourer. Occupation: Labourer. Enlistment location: St Helen's, Lancashire. Killed in action, France & Flanders, 30 December 1917. Age: 22. Memorial: Panel 92 to 93 and 162A, Tyne Cot Memorial.

FINEGAN, William: Private, Leinster Regiment, 2nd Battalion, 7875. Born: Donore. Enlistment location: Drogheda. Served in France from 8 September 1914. Killed in action. France & Flanders, 20 October 1914. First battle of the 2nd Battalion, took place 18-20 October 1914 at Armentieres. Memorial: Panel 10, Ploegsteert Memorial, Comines-Warneton, Hainaut. Drogheda War Memorial.

FINNEGAN, Thomas J.: Private, Leinster Regiment, 1st Battalion, 4566. Baptised: Trim, 1 May 1897. Son of Thomas and Bridget Finnegan, *née* Rochfort, Seaton Lane, later of St Loman Street and later of Wellington Street, Trim. Father's occupation: Labourer. Enlistment location: Drogheda. Died of wounds, Egypt, 17 March 1918. Age 21. Memorial: Plot Q, Grave 70, Jerusalem War Cemetery. From Trim Church of Ireland, Roll of Honour, 'Finnegan, T. Private, Leinster Regiment.' From the *Meath Chronicle*, 25 May 1918, 'Private T. Finnegan (Leinsters), of Trim, is officially reported killed in action.'

FITZPATRICK, Edward: Rifleman, The London Regiment, (Post Office Rifles), 8th Battalion, 372568. Baptised: Johnstown, 6 April 1894. Son of Thomas and Rose Fitzpatrick, *née* Halton, Kilcarn. Killed in action, France & Flanders, 5 March 1917. Memorial: B.5, Bailleumont Communal Cemetery.

FITZPATRICK, Patrick: Sapper, Royal Engineers, 36480. Son of Martin and Elizabeth Fitzpatrick, *née* Smith. Father's occupation: Labourer in Brickworks. Occupation: General Labourer. Husband of Teresa Fitzpatrick, *née* Hickey, Rathdrina, Beauparc. Three children. Enlisted: 4 January 1916. Enlistment location: Navan. Died at home of Landry's Paralysis, 29 December 1919. Age: 32. Memorial: Knockcommon Cemetery.

FITZSIMONS, Frank: Rifleman, Royal Irish Rifles, 1st Garrison Battalion, G/1058. Formerly Royal Dublin Fusiliers, 18810. Baptised: Navan, 4 March 1883. Son of Thomas and Bridget Fitzsimons, *née* Clarke, Athlumney. Father's occupation: General Labourer. Residence: Gorey, Co. Wexford. Enlistment location: Naas, Co. Kildare. Died: India, 13 May 1916. Buried in Cawnpore Cantonment New Cemetery. Memorial: Face 23, Madras 1914-1918 War Memorial, Chennai.

FLANAGAN, James: Private, Royal Dublin Fusiliers, 2nd Battalion, 20258. Baptised: Navan, 6 May 1895. Son of Patrick and Mary Flanagan, *née* Fitzsimons, Academy Street, Navan. Father's occupation: Shoemaker. Occupation: (1911) Apprentice in woollen mill. Residence: Navan. Enlistment location: Dublin. Killed in action, France & Flanders, 1 July 1916. First day of the Battle of the Somme. Age: 21. Memorial: B.57, Redan Ridge Cemetery No. 2, Beaumont-Hamel. Old Athlumney graveyard.

FLOOD, Michael Joseph: Corporal, Royal Irish Rifles, 7th Battalion, 4564. Born: Slane, 8 February 1899. Son of Thomas and Ellen F. Flood, *née* Downey, Slane. Father's occupation: Draper. Enlistment location: Slane. Served in France from 15 December 1915. Killed in action, France & Flanders, 16 August 1917. Memorial: Panel 138 to 140 and 162 to 162A and 163A, Tyne Cot Memorial. From the *Meath Chronicle*, 1 September 1917, 'Intelligence has reached his parents during the week of the death in action on the 16th ult. of Lance-Corporal Michael Flood, of R.I.R., a native of Slane.'

FLOOD, Patrick: Sapper, Royal Engineers, 180th Tunnelling Company. 359658. Formerly Royal Irish Rifles, 7/3942. Born: Slane. Son of Patrick and Mary Flood, Coalpits, Slane. Father's Occupation: Agricultural Labourer. Occupation: (1901)

Agricultural Labourer, (1911) Copper Miner. Residence: Slane. Enlistment location: Drogheda. Died of wounds, General Hospital 10, France, 6 April 1918. Age: 40. Memorial: P.VII.I.9B, St Sever Cemetery Extension, Rouen.

FLYNN, Patrick: Sapper, Royal Engineers, 3rd Field Survey Company. 165918. Born: Longwood. Enlistment location: Battersea, Surrey. Died of wounds, France & Flanders, 26 September 1918. Memorial: B.22, Queant Communal Cemetery British Extension.

FOLEY, Christopher: Gunner, Royal Field Artillery, 504th Battery, 65th Brigade, 197207. Formerly Horse Keeper, S.E. 15597, Royal Army Veterinary Corps. Born: Meath. Son of Patrick and Bridget Foley, Dunshaughlin. Father's Occupation: Publican. Occupation: Farmer's son. Enlistment location: Woolwich. Died: France & Flanders, 10 August 1918. Age: 26. Memorial: IV.A.17, Aire Communal Cemetery.

FORAN, John: Private, Irish Guards, 1st Battalion, 9605. Born: Boardsmill. Enlistment location: Trim. Killed in action, France & Flanders, 30 March 1918. Memorial: IV.J.6, Douchy-les-Ayette British Cemetery. From Trim Church of Ireland, Roll of Honour, 'Foran, J. Private, Irish Guards.'

FORTUNE, Christopher: Private, Royal Irish Fusiliers, 8th Battalion, 21060. Formerly Connaught Rangers, 3926. Baptised: Ratoath, 30 December 1895. Son of Edward and Mary Fortune, née Murphy, Ratoath. Father's occupation: Farm Labourer. Occupation: Labourer. Residence: Ratoath. Enlistment location: Dublin. Killed in the second battle of Ypres. A personal friend of the poet, Francis Ledwidge, who was killed at the third battle of Ypres. Killed in action, Ypres, 25 April 1916. Age: 20. Memorial: Sp. Mem. 5, Vermelles British Cemetery.

FOWLER, George Glyn: Second Lieutenant, King's Royal Rifle Corps, 2nd Battalion. Born: 21 January 1896. Younger son of Captain and Mrs R.H. Fowler, of Rahinston, Enfield. Father's occupation: Retired Army Captain and JP. Served in France from 26 January 1915. Died of wounds received at the Battle of Loos, 26 September 1915. Age: 19. Memorial: I.C.52, Lapugnoy Military Cemetery. His brother, Robert St Leger Fowler, served as a captain in the First World War, winning a Military Cross during the defence of Amiens against the last German offensive of 1918. Robert died from leukaemia at Rahinstown in 1925. From a tablet in Rathmolyon church, 'George Glyn Fowler, Lieutenant K.R.R.C., born 21 Jan 1896, died of wounds 26 Sept 1915.' From a tablet in church at lectern, 'To the glory of God and in most loving memory of Lieutenant George Glyn Fowler, 60th Rifles, who gave his life for his country on September 26th 1915 at Loos Aged 19.' From wooden cross on south wall, 'Lt George Glyn Fowler, 1st Bn K.R.R.C. died of wounds in the battle of Loos 25th September 1915 aged 19.' This cross was moved from the grave at Lapugnoy Military Cemetery (Plot 1 Row C Grave 52) when the permanent headstone was erected. From Trim Church of Ireland, Roll of Honour, '2nd Lt. G.G. Fowler 60th Rifles K.R.R.' From the *Meath Chronicle*, 9 October 1915:

Trim Rural Council
Fell in the War
Mr. Ennis proposed: – The Trim District Council desire to express to Capt. and Mrs Fowler of Rahinstown, their deep sympathy on the death of their son, Lieut. George St L. Fowler.

Mr. Shannon said that he seconded the resolution with regret. It was more than sad to see such a fine type of manhood taken away. He wished to join in the expression of sympathy with Capt. and Mrs Fowler.

The Chairman, Mr. King and Mr. Maguire associated themselves with the resolution which was passed.

FOX, Patrick: Private, Irish Guards, 1st Battalion, 5861. Baptised: Navan, 29 December 1874. Son of Patrick and Joan Fox, *née* Crahan, Flower Hill, Navan. Father's occupation: Labourer. Enlistment location: Navan. Served in France from 24 May 1915. Killed in action, France & Flanders, 15 September 1916. Age: 40. Memorial: Pier and Face 7D, Thiepval Memorial. From the *Meath Chronicle*, 31 July 1915, 'At the Navan recruiting meeting Mr. Timmon stated that he had a letter from Mr. P. Fox, who was once a "back" in the Pierce Mahony's but is now a "forward" at the front scoring points for the English!' See M.J. Colclough's letter. From the *Meath Chronicle*, 28 October 1916, 'News has reached Navan that Private Patk. Fox, Irish Guards, has been killed in action. He was one of the old Pierce Mahony football club.' From the *Meath Chronicle*, 4 November 1916, 'News of the death of Pte. Patrick Fox, 1st Batt, Irish Guards, has reached Navan, his native town and aroused much regret amongst his companions and friends. He was killed in action on September 25. His mother and friends reside at Flower Hill.'

FURLONG, Patrick: Lance-Sergeant, Royal Dublin Fusiliers, 6th Battalion, 15818. Baptised: Enfield, 6 May 1891. Son of John and Jane Furlong, *née* Daly, New Lodge, Clegarrow, Enfield. Father's occupation: Bricklayer, Stone Mason. Occupation: Stone Mason. Residence: Enfield. Enlisted: Curragh Camp. Served in Balkans from 7 August 1915. Died of wounds, Balkans, 29 March 1916. Age: 26. Memorial: I.B.I, Sofia War Cemetery.

G

GAFFNEY, John: Private, South Lancashire Regiment, 7th Battalion, 15063. Born: Oldcastle. Son of Peter and Elizabeth Gaffney, Ross. Residence: Ross, Mountnugent. Occupation: Excavator. Enlistment location: Horwich, Lancashire, 5 October 1915, aged 38 years. Height: 5 foot 8¾ inches. Eyes: Blue. Hair: Brown. Served at home from October 1914 to July 1915. Served in France from 18 July 1915. Killed in action, France & Flanders, 18 November 1916. Memorial: Pier and Face 7A and 7B, Thiepval Memorial.

GAFFNEY, Richard: Private, Leinster Regiment, 7th Battalion, 5086. Born: Collinstown, Co. Westmeath. Residence: Collinstown, Co. Westmeath. Enlistment location: Athboy. Served in France from 17 December 1915. Killed in action, France & Flanders, 19 April 1916. Memorial: II.L.38, Vermelles British Cemetery. From the *Meath Chronicle*, 20 May 1916, 'Intelligence has reached Athboy that Private Gaffney of the Leinster Regiment, has fallen in Flanders. He was in the employment of Mr. Byrne, druggist, Athboy, prior to the outbreak of the war.'

GAISFORD, Robert Sandeman: Captain, Royal Flying Corps, 34th Squadron, Secondary Regiment: Royal Field Artillery. Born: Guilsfield, Montgomeryshire, 14 January 1896. Son of Lieutenant Colonel and Mrs D.J. Gaisford, Dollys Grove, Dunboyne, Co. Meath. Older brother, John William Gaisford, joined the Royal Artillery on 17 November 1914, was wounded in Gallipoli but survived the war. Commissioned as a Second Lieutenant in the RFA on 16 September 1914. Promoted Lieutenant 9 June 1915. Received Royal Aero Club Aviators' Certificate on Maurice Farman Biplane at Military School, Ruislip on 7 June 1917. Seconded to the RFC on 4 August 1917 in the temporary rank of Captain for employment as a Flight Commander. Promoted to Captain on 1 January 1918. Killed over enemy lines, Italy, when engaged with four hostile machines, 30 January 1918. The aeroplane was shot down in flames by Austro-Hungarian anti-aircraft fire over the Piave Sector of the Italian Front on either 29 or 30 January 1918. The RE 8 crashed east of Nervesa and both airmen were killed. Memorial: Plot 5, Row B, Grave 6, Tezze British Cemetery.

GALLIGAN, Patrick: Private, Leinster Regiment, 7th Battalion, 1399. Baptised: Navan, 13 June 1887. Son of Laurence and Julia Galligan, *née* Byrne, Mill Lane, Navan. Father's occupation: Baker. Occupation: General Labourer.

Enlistment location: Navan. Served in France from 17 December 1915. Killed in action, France & Flanders, 8 March 1917. Memorial: Panel 44, Ypres (Menin Gate) Memorial.

GALLIGAN, Thomas: Private, Leinster Regiment, 2nd Battalion, 4733. Baptised: Navan, 3 January 1895. Son of Laurence and Julia Galligan, *née* Byrne, Barrack Lane, Navan. Father's occupation: Baker. Occupation: General Labourer. Enlistment location: Navan. Served in France from 26 October 1914. Died of wounds, 13 August 1915 Age: 19. Memorial: III. D. 27, Lijssenthoek Military Cemetery.

GANNON, James: Private, Royal Irish Regiment, 7th Battalion, 25313. Formerly South Irish Horse, 2102. Born: Dunboyne. Baptised: Kilcloon, 18 November 1891. Son of Daniel and Catherine Gannon, *née* Martin, Brownrath and later of Quarryland, Dunboyne. Father's occupation: Shepherd. Occupation: Farm Servant. Residence: Dunboyne. Enlistment location: Dublin. Killed in action, France & Flanders, 21 March 1918. Memorial: Panel 30 and 31, Pozieres Memorial.

GANNON, William: Private, Royal Irish Regiment, 2nd Battalion, 5122. Baptised: Ballivor, 10 March 1889. Son of Michael and Elizabeth Gannon, *née* Kiernan, Ballivor and later of Patrick Street, Athlone, Co. Westmeath.

Residence: Warrentown, Co. Meath. Enlistment location: Boyle, Co. Roscommon. Killed in action, France & Flanders, 21 March 1918. Age: 29. Memorial: Panel 30 and 31, Pozieres Memorial.

GAUGHRAN, Christopher: Sergeant, Royal Garrison Artillery. 28857. Baptised: Trim, 24 December 1889. Son of James and Margaret Gaughran, *née* Blake, Corporationland North, Trim. Father's occupation: Farmer. Died: Trim, 16 November 1918. Award: Military Medal. Memorial: Newtown Cemetery, Trim. From Newtown Cemetery, Trim, 'Pray for the soul of Christopher Gaughran, Trim, who died 16th November 1918 aged 29 years. Erected in remembrance by his comrades of the 200 Siege Battery RCA.'

GAUGHRAN, John: From the *Meath Chronicle*, 3 October 1914: 'Oldcastle Men killed in the War. Deep regret has been occasioned in the Oldcastle district by the news that John Gaughran, Ballinlough; Private Smith, Fennor and Joseph Bergin, Oldcastle have been killed in the war.'

GAUGHRAN, Thomas: Private, Royal Dublin Fusiliers, 6th Battalion, 23596. Baptised: Ballinlough, 22 June 1884. Son of Thomas and Rose Gaughran, *née* Farrelly, Ballinlough Big. Father's occupation: Shepherd. Residence: Ballinlough. Enlistment location: Sutton, Co. Dublin. Killed in action, France & Flanders, 8 October 1918. Memorial: III.C.16, Prospect Hill Cemetery, Gouy.

GAVIN, James: Private, Royal Irish Fusiliers, 2nd Battalion, 17476. Baptised: Duleek, 12 July 1896. Son of Thomas and Mary Ann Gavin, *née* Whyte, Platten, Duleek, and later Donore Road, Drogheda. Occupation: (1911) Farm Servant. Enlistment location: Drogheda, January 1915. Killed in action, France & Flanders, 5 May 1915. Age: 19. Memorial: Panel 42, Ypres (Menin Gate) Memorial. Donore Graveyard.

GEOGHEGAN, Michael: Private, Royal Irish Fusiliers, 7th/8th Battalion, 15971. Residence: Kells. Enlistment location: Tipperary. Died: France & Flanders, 6 April 1917.

GERAGHTY, Patrick: Private, Connaught Rangers, 2nd Battalion, 8299. Baptised: Kells, 23 May 1880. Son of James and Mary Anne Geraghty, *née* Dixon, Church Lane, Kells. Father's occupation: Butcher. Occupation: Labourer. Residence: Kells. Enlistment location: Dublin. Killed in action, France & Flanders, 14 September 1914. Memorial: II.E.12, Vailly British Cemetery. From the *Meath Chronicle*; 17 October 1914:

Kells Soldier Missing
On Thursday news reached Kells that a native of the town, Patrick Geraghty of the Connaught Rangers, serving in France, had been killed in the war.

We are glad to learn that so far the report has not been verified. A telegram from the War Office, received by his sister yesterday evening, states that he is missing since September 19th. Geraghty was a well-conducted and industrious lad and his comrades and friends would be glad to learn of his safety.

From the *Meath Chronicle*, 7 November 1914:

Kells Man killed in the War
Word has reached Kells from the War Office that Patrick Geraghty, of Kells, who was serving in the war with the Connaught Rangers, was shot dead on September 14th. All who knew the deceased deeply regret the sad event. In the notification a message of deep sympathy with his relatives was enclosed from the King and Queen.

From the *Meath Chronicle*, 13 February 1915:

Kell's Soldier's Death
A letter addressed to Mr. James Geraghty, Church Lane, Kells has been received from the captain in charge of the Record Office in Cork giving particu-

lars of the death and burial of Private Patrick Geraghty of the 2nd Connaught Rangers, who was killed in action at Soupier Hill on September 14th, 1914. He was found at the top of Soupier Hill together with Grenadier, Coldstream and Irish Guardsmen and Connaught Rangers and a cross was erected to mark the grave. Poor Geraghty who was a reservist left Kells on August 9th to rejoin his regiment.

GERRARD, Christopher: Private, South Lancashire Regiment, 2nd Battalion, 17709. Formerly Lancashire Fusiliers, 4794. Baptised: Bohermeen, 9 December 1882. Son of Thomas and Anne Gerrard, *née* Fitzsimons, White Quarry, Ardbraccan, Navan. Mother's occupation: Farmer. Occupation: (1901) General Labourer. Occupation at enlistment: Collier. Enlistment location: Wigan, Lancashire, 30 August 1914. Height: 5 foot 8¾ inches. Complexion: Pale. Eyes: Blue. Hair: Black. Served in France from 2 April 1915. Died of wounds, 9th General Hospital, Rouen, France, 21 July 1916. Age: 33. Memorial: A.36.7, St Sever Cemetery, Rouen.

GIBBONS, Patrick: Private, Royal Dublin Fusiliers, 2nd Battalion, 11701. Born: Trim. Residence: Trim. Enlistment location: Naas. Served in France from 27 October 1914. Killed in action, France & Flanders, 25 April 1915. Memorial: Panel 44 and 46, Ypres (Menin Gate) Memorial.

GIBNEY, John: Driver, 183rd Infantry Brigade HQ, Army Service Corps, T2/015273. Baptised: Trim, 2 February 1879. Son of John and Mary Gibney, *née* Clarke. Husband of Honora Annie Gibney, The Bungalow, Lenzie, Glasgow. Residence: Lenzie, Glasgow. Enlisted: 9 October 1914. Age given on enlistment: 28. Enlistment location: Inverkeithing. Died in hospital while undergoing operation, Egypt, 12 September 1918. Age: 40. Memorial: C.93, Alexandria (Hadra) War Memorial Cemetery, Egypt.

GIBNEY, James: Petty Officer 1st Class, Royal Navy, HMS *Defence*. 193687. Baptised: Oldcastle, 6 July 1881. Son of James and Marcella Gibney, *née* Tuite, Lennox Street, Oldcastle. Father's occupation: Publican and Shopkeeper. Gibney made the highest individual score with Light Quick Firing Guns in the Fleet in 1910; and he passed the professional and educational examinations for Gunner (Warrant Officer) in 1915. Died: 31 May 1916. Age: 35. Memorial: 11, Plymouth Naval Memorial. From the *Meath Chronicle*, 17 June 1916:

Oldcastle Seaman lost in Naval Fight
Deep sympathy is felt by the people of Oldcastle for Mrs Gibney on the death of her son,

James Gibney, who was one of the crew of HMS Defence, lost in the great battle of Jutland in the North Sea. Mr. Gibney, who was aged 34 years, was one of the crack gunners of the British Navy. Some time ago we published an account of a test held at the China Station, on which occasion he made the highest percentage of hits and was declared champion of the station. He was also a pugilist of rare ability, and held the middle-weight boxing championship of the navy. A young man of splendid physique, he was of bright and genial manner and made hosts of friends everywhere he went. It is sad to see a career so promising cut short in the bloom of manhood.

GIBNEY, John: Private, Leinster Regiment, 1st Battalion, 8535. Born: Duleek. Enlistment location: Drogheda. Brother of Miss Margaret Joseph Gibney, 11 Summer Hill, Killarney, Co. Kerry. Served in France from 19 December 1914. Killed in action, France & Flanders, 14 February 1915. Memorial: Panel 44, Ypres (Menin Gate) Memorial. Drogheda War Memorial.

GIBSON, Walter David: Rifleman, Royal Irish Rifles, 14th Battalion, 18/1730. Born: Oldcastle. Residence: (1901) Drakestown, Castletown (at enlistment) Devonport. Enlisted:

Plymouth, Devon. Died of wounds, France & Flanders, 20 August 1917. Age: 27. Memorial: VIII. I. 10, Boulogne Eastern Cemetery.

GILBERT, James: Acting-Wheeler-Corporal, Royal Army Service Corps, 866th H.T. Company. TS/9494. Born: Navan or Wiltshire. Son of William and Sarah Gilbert. Husband of Alice Gilbert, Alpha Cottage, High Street, Crowthorne, Berkshire. Residence: Crowthorne, Berkshire. Enlistment location: Camberley, Surrey. Died: home, 10 October 1918. Age: 42. Memorial: Hollybrook Memorial, Southampton.

GILES, Victor Marshall: Second Lieutenant, Royal Irish Rifles 7th Battalion. Baptised: Navan, 26 March 1897. Son of Marshall and Ethel Giles, *née* Carver, Brewshill, Navan and later of 66 University Street, Belfast. Father's occupation: Bookkeeper at F. & J. Clayton & Co. Ltd. Entered Blue Coat School in 1911 as King's Scholar. Left 1914. He relinquished a valuable scholarship at King's Hospital in order to serve. Served in France from 29 December 1915. Killed in action, France & Flanders, 28 June 1916. Age: 19. Memorial: IV. A. 13, Vermelles British Cemetery. Roll of Honour, St Mary's church, Navan.

GILLIAT, Cecil ('Glennie') Glendower Percival: Captain, Royal Warwickshire Regiment, 1st Battalion,

Eldest son of Cecil Gilliat, Arch Hall, Co. Meath. Born: 6 December 1884. Educated: Cheltenham. Gazetted Second Lieutenant, Royal Warwickshire Regiment from the Militia, 29 November 1905. Promoted Lieutenant 1 April 1909 and Captain, posthumously, 29 October 1914, ante-dated to 12 September previously. Served on the north-west Frontier of India 1908, Medal with clasp. Died of wounds, 14 October 1914. Age: 29. Memorial: II. D. 39, Hazebrouck Communal Cemetery. From the *Meath Chronicle*, 28 November 1914: 'Meathmen Killed and Wounded. Mr. Gilliatt of Archall and Private Wm. Kenny, O'Growney Terrace, Navan of the Dublin Fusiliers, are also reported to have been killed.'

GILLIAT, Reginald Horace Crosbie: Captain, Leinster Regiment, 5th Battalion, Attached to the Connaught Rangers, 1st Battalion, formerly 2nd Battalion. Son of Cecil Gilliat, Arch Hall, Co. Meath and New Club, Cheltenham, Gloucestershire. Served in France from 17 October 1914. Killed in action, 6 April 1915. Memorial: I.A.18, Rue-du-Bacquerot No. 1 Military Cemetery, Laventie. 'Reginald H. Gilliatt, Captain, Leinster Regiment killed in action at Neuve Chapelle 6 April 1915' (Julianstown church, stained-glass window).

GILSENAN, Thomas: Stoker. 1st Class, Royal Navy, HMS *Suffolk*. SS/110420. Baptised: Oristown, 22 September 1888. Son of John and Mary Gilsenan, *née* Healy, Kilberry, Navan. Father's occupation: Agricultural Labourer. Died: 13 October 1915. Age: 28. Memorial: 95, Bermuda Royal Naval Cemetery.

GLANCY, James: Corporal, Northumberland Fusiliers, 18th Battalion, Tyneside Pioneers, 59393. Formerly Army Service Corps, 062595. Born: Durrow, Queen's County. Son of Bartley and Jemima Glancy, Ballinlough House, Kells. Father's occupation: Gamekeeper. Enlisted: Latham Park, Lancashire. Served in France from 26 March 1915. Died: France & Flanders, 17 April 1918. Age: 29. Memorial: XXVII.G.16A, Lijssenthoek Military Cemetery. From War Memorial, 1914-1918, Kells Church of Ireland, 'Private J. Glancy, Northumberland Fus.'

GLYNN, John: Corporal, Leinster Regiment, 2nd Battalion, 397. Baptised: Athboy, 19 July 1892. Son of Robert and Mary Jane Glynn. Father's occupation: Coachman. Enlistment location: Carlow. Served in France from 1 April 1915. Died of wounds, France & Flanders, 22 August 1916. Age: 24. Memorial: 11.A.45, La Neuville British Cemetery.

GOGARTY, Christopher: Guardsman, Guards' Machine Gun Regiment, 4th Battalion, 1878.

Formerly Irish Guards, 6551. Born: Trim. Son of William and Jane Gogarty, Brannoxtown, Trim. Father's occupation: Shepherd. Residence: Trim. Occupation: Farm Servant. Enlisted: January 1915. Enlistment location: Drogheda. Served in France from 16 August 1915. Wounded at Loos in September 1915. Hospitalised in England and returned to the Front in 1916. Transferred to the Machine Gun Guards in February 1918. Died of wounds, Doullens Casualty Clearing Station, France, 30 March 1918. Age: 26. Memorial: VI.F.8, Doullens Communal Cemetery Extension No. 1.

GOGARTY, Matthew: Private, Royal Dublin Fusiliers, 1st Battalion, 25342. Born: Duleek. Husband of Mrs Annie Gogarty, Corballis, Drogheda, Co. Meath; later of Streamstown, Co. Westmeath. Residence: Duleek. Enlistment location: Drogheda. Died of wounds, France & Flanders, 14 October 1918. Memorial: VI.E.37, Dadizeele New British Cemetery. Drogheda War Memorial.

GORMAN, James: Gunner, Royal Marine Artillery, Siege Guns (Dunkerque) RMA/13718. Baptised: Duleek, 30 May 1892. Son of James and Agnes Gorman, née Bird, King's Gate, Commons, Duleek. Father's occupation: Labourer. Occupation: Agricultural Labourer. Died 25 September 1918. Age 25. Memorial: II.K.16, Coxyde Military Cemetery. Drogheda War Memorial.

GORMAN, Joseph Patrick: Lance-Corporal, Royal Irish Rifles, 1st Battalion, 8925. Baptised: Navan, 28 March 1881. Son of John and Catherine Gorman, née Caffrey, Brews Hill. Father's occupation: Cord Wainer and later Shoemaker. Occupation: (1901) Labourer in Flour Mill, (1911) General Labourer. Enlistment location: Navan. Killed in action, France & Flanders, 1 July 1916. First day of the Battle of the Somme. Memorial: Pier and Face 15A and 15B, Thiepval Memorial.

GOUGH, Patrick: Private, Leinster Regiment, 2nd Battalion, 5930. Born: Stamullin. Enlistment location: Mosney. Died of wounds, France & Flanders, 23 April 1918. Memorial: P.VI.F.2A, St Sever Cemetery Extension, Rouen.

GRADWELL, George Francis: Second Lieutenant, Royal Dublin Fusiliers, 1st Battalion. Son of George Fitzgerald Gradwell, Platten Hall, Meath and Sarah, eldest daughter of Francis William Leland, Littlegrange, Co. Louth. Residence: Paradise Place, Drogheda, Co. Louth. Born 29 November 1898. Educated: St George's College, Weybridge. Killed in action, Sailly-Saillesel, 28 February 1917. Age: 18. Memorial: Pier and Face 16C, Thiepval Memorial. Drogheda War Memorial.

GRAHAM: From the *Meath Chronicle*, 15 July 1916, 'Private Graham, Navan, of the Leinster Regiment, died in hospital on Tuesday last after a lingering illness.'

GREY, George Rochfort: Private, Dorset Queen's Own Yeomanry, 1st/1st, H/73062. Formerly South Irish Horse. Baptised: Athboy, 21 September 1891. Son of George and Mary Grey, *née* Lyster, Athboy and later of 102 Cabra Park, Phibsborough, Dublin. Enlistment location: Dublin. Died of pneumonia, on active service, Palestine, 11 October 1918. Age: 27. Memorial: B.2, Haifa War Cemetery.

GRIFFIN, James: Private, Leinster Regiment, 2nd Battalion, 10677. Born: Kells. Enlistment location: Navan. Killed in action, France & Flanders, 21 March 1918. Memorial: Panel 78, Pozieres Memorial.

GRIFFIN, P.: Royal Irish Fusiliers From the *Meath Chronicle*, 21 October 1916, 'Local Soldiers Killed. The following local soldiers are reported to have been recently killed: Pte. P. Reilly, Irish Guards (Navan) and Pte. P. Griffin, Royal Irish Fusiliers (Navan).'

GRIFFIN, Thomas: Private, Royal Irish Fusiliers, 8th Battalion, 21423. Born: Killinkere, Co. Cavan. Son of Sam and Annie Griffin, Fennor, Painestown and later of Athboy. Father's occupation: Shepherd and Agricultural Labourer. Residence: Wilkinstown, Co. Meath. Enlistment location: Cavan. Killed in action, 4 September 1916. Age: 16. Memorial: Sp. Mem. 27, Flatiron Copse Cemetery, Mametz.

GRIFFITH, George Hartley: Private, Royal Irish Regiment, 5th Battalion, 145. Baptised: Trim, 18 February 1876. Son of Francis and Margaret Griffith. Father's occupation: (1876) Turnkey at Trim Gaol, (1911) Church Sexton. His brother, Henry John, was also killed in the war. Residence: Poolboy Street, Navan. Enlistment location: Clonmel, Co. Tipperary. Died, home, 10 October 1914. Age: 37. Memorial: RC.432, Grangegorman Military Cemetery.

GRIFFITH, Henry John: Lance-Sergeant, Royal Dublin Fusiliers, 8th Battalion, 19898. Born: Bailieboro, Co. Cavan. Son of Francis and Margaret Griffith, Navan. Husband of Annie Griffith, 6 Hudson's Terrace, Bray, Co. Wicklow. Father's occupation: (1876) Turnkey at Trim Gaol, (1911) Church Sexton. His brother, George Hartley, was also killed in the war. Enlistment location: Bray, Co. Wicklow. Died of wounds, Proven, France, 7 August 1917. Age: 36. Memorial: IV.A.30, Mendinghem Military Cemetery. Roll of Honour, St Mary's church, Navan.

H

HAGERTY, James: Private, Irish Guards, 2nd Battalion, 8197. Nobber. Born about 1880. Entered Wilson's Hospital School, 1891. Husband of Annie Kate Hagerty, Castle Kieran, Carnaross, Kells. Residence: Castle Kiernan, Carnaross. Enlistment location: Dublin. Died of wounds, 14 or 15 September 1916. Age: 37. Memorial: II.D.64, La Neuvelle British Cemetery, Corbie. Drogheda War Memorial.

HALLIGAN, John: Private, Leinster Regiment, B Company, 2nd Battalion, 4734. Born: Co. Offaly. Son of John and Kate Halligan, Sarsfield Avenue, Church Street, Trim. Residence: Trim. Enlistment location: Drogheda. Served in France from 4 April 1915. Killed in action, France & Flanders, 8 June 1915. Age: 19. Memorial: B.6A, La Brique Military Cemetery No. 1. From Trim Church of Ireland, Roll of Honour, 'Halligan, J. Private, Leinster Regiment.'

HALLIGAN, Richard: Private, Leinster Regiment, 2nd Battalion, 10085. Born: Co. Kilkenny. Residence: Trim. Son of Catherine Halligan, 6 Newtown, Clonbun, Trim. Occupation: Servant. Enlistment location: Drogheda. Served in France from 8 September 1914. Killed in action, France & Flanders, 20 October 1914. First battle of the 2nd Battalion, took place 18-20 October 1914 at Armentieres. Age: 19. Memorial: Panel 10, Ploegsteert Memorial. From Trim Church of Ireland, Roll of Honour, 'Halligan, R. Private, Leinster Regiment.'

HALPIN, Edward: Private, Royal Irish Regiment, 2nd Battalion, 5799. Born: Killary. Baptised: Lobinstown, 28 April 1891. Husband of Mrs A. Halpin, 24 Ferrant Street, Widnes, Lancashire. Enlisted: 28 December 1916. Enlistment location: Widnes, Lancashire. Age at enlistment: 23. Killed in action, France & Flanders, 27 July 1917. Memorial: I.T.6, Menin Road South Military Cemetery.

HALPIN, John: Private, Royal Irish Regiment, 2nd Battalion, 5798. Baptised: Lobinstown, 8 April 1889. Son of John and Anne Halpin, *née* Lynch, Killary, Lobinstown, Slane. Father's occupation: Agricultural Labourer. Occupation: Agricultural Labourer. Enlistment location: Widnes, Lancashire. Killed in action, France & Flanders, 7 June 1917. Age: 27. Memorial: I.E.2, Wytschaete Military Cemetery.

HALPIN, Matthew: Private. Royal Inniskilling Fusiliers, 8th Battalion, 25476. Transferred to 30th Labour Group HQ, 421203. Son of Matthew and Mary Halpin, Barristown, Slane. Husband of Hannah Halpin, 105 Butler Street, Belfast. Occupation: (1911) General Labourer. Died of broncho pneumonia, 27 February 1919. Age: 32. Memorial: V.F.41, Longuenesse (St Omer) Souvenir Cemetery.

HALTON, Mathew: Private, Irish Guards, 1st Battalion, 1850. Baptised: Kilbride, Dunderry parish, 1 November 1881. Son of Michael and Bridget Halton, *née* Bligh, Clonfane, Trim. Father's occupation: Farmer. Enlistment location: Dublin. Served in France from 13 February 1915. Died of wounds, France & Flanders, 6 August 1916. Age: 34. Buried in Tullaghanoge Graveyard, Trim. Memorial: Panel 4 (Screen Wall), Grangegorman Memorial.

HAMILTON, Andrew: Private, Royal Dublin Fusiliers, 2nd Battalion, 24796. Born: Ardcath, about 1889. Son of Nicholas and Catherine Hamilton, Cloghan, Ardcath. Residence: Ardcath. Father's occupation: Agricultural Labourer. Enlistment location: Drogheda. Killed in action, France & Flanders, 1st July 1916. First day of the Battle of the Somme. Memorial: Pier and Face 16 C, Thiepval Memorial.

HAMILTON, Lawrence: Stoker, Royal Naval Reserve, HMS *Black Prince*, 4478S. Baptised: Johnstown, 30 April 1877. Son of John and Ellen Hamilton, *née* Murray, Dean Hill, Navan. Mother's occupation: Domestic Servant. Killed in action at Battle of Jutland, 31 May 1916. Age: 30. Memorial: 19, Plymouth Naval Memorial.

HAMMICK, St Vincent Charles Farrant: Gentleman Cadet. Royal Military College, E Company, Sandhurst. Born: Dublin. Had served in the Motor Transport Section of the Trinity College Dublin Officer Training Corps. Son of Revd. C.H.W. Hammick and Mrs A.M.C. Hammick, The Rectory, Slane. Father: Charles Horatio Walter Hammick was born in South Africa in 1866, educated at Trinity College and became Assistant Master at Drogheda Grammer School in 1897. Revd Hammick served as curate in St Mary's, Drogheda 1904-6, incumbent of Duleek from 1906 to 1932, to which Slane was added in 1928. In 1911 Revd Hammick lived at Palace Street, Drogheda. He was incumbent of Trim from 1932 until his death a year later in 1933. St Vincent Charles Farrant Hammick died at Sandhurst, of measles, 6 March 1917. Age: 21. Memorial: 551, Sandhurst Royal Military Academy Cemetery. Drogheda War Memorial.

HANLEY, Owen: Private, Royal Dublin Fusiliers, 2nd Battalion, 11615. Born: Kilmessan. Residence: Rathcoole, Co. Dublin. Enlistment location: Naas. Served in France from

23 August 1914. Killed in action, France & Flanders, 20 November 1914. Memorial: Panel 10, Ploegsteert Memorial.

HARLIN, Arthur Joseph: Lance-Corporal, Royal Munster Fusiliers, 1ˢᵗ Battalion, 18064. Formerly Royal Irish Fusiliers, 18605. Baptised: Navan, 15 April 1891. Son of John and Mary Anne Harlin, *née* Gearty, Chapel Street and later of 53 Margate Road, Southsea, England. Residence: Dublin. Enlistment location: Dublin. Killed in action, France & Flanders, 30 September 1918.

HAROLD, Thomas Francis: Private, Australian Infantry, AIF, 25ᵗʰ Battalion, 1934. Baptised: Navan, 12 February 1889. Son of James and Mary Anne Harold, *née* Pentleton, Cornmarket, Navan. Father's occupation: Dealer. Occupation: Fitter. Enlisted: 17 June 1915. Enlistment location: Brisbane. Height: 5 foot 5 inches. Eyes: Brown. Hair: Light Brown. Served in Gallipoli from 12 October 1915. Served in France from 19 March 1916. Killed in action, France & Flanders, 29 July 1916. Age: 25. Memorial: Villers-Bretonneux Memorial.

HATCH, Nicholas Stephen: Second Lieutenant, Royal Irish Rifles. 13ᵗʰ Battalion. Baptised: Duleek, 26 December 1895. Son of Mark and Jemima Hatch, Millhouse, Duleek.

Father's occupation: Farmer. Served in France from 13 February 1916. Killed in action, 1 July 1916. First day of the Battle of the Somme. Age: 20. Memorial: X.A.1, AIF Burial Ground, Flers, Somme. Drogheda War Memorial.

HEALY, Guy Rambaut: Lieutenant, Royal Munster Fusiliers, 4ᵗʰ Battalion, Attached to King's African Rifles, 3ʳᵈ Battalion. Son of Archdeacon John and Mary Healy, Kells. Revd John Healy was incumbent of Kells from 1887 to 1917, archdeacon of Meath from 1914 to 1928, a Prebandry of St Patrick's Cathedral, Dublin from 1898 to 1935 and Treasurer of St Patrick's Cathedral, Dublin from 1935 to 1942. Revd Healy wrote *History of the Diocese of Meath* which was published in two volumes in 1908. Guy Rambaut Healy was husband of Mrs G.R. Healy, Thormanby, Howth, Co. Dublin. Healy served in the Boer War. Served in British East Africa from June 1915. Killed in action, Lateema Hill, East Africa, while taking part in General Smut's engagement at Kitovo, 11 March 1916. Age: 33. Memorial: IX.A.1, Taveta Military Cemetery. From north window of Kells church, 'Artist: Heaton, Butler & Bayne, London.' Subject: 'A Good Wife' (Proverbs 31:27) and 'Armour of God' (Ephesians 6:11). 'She looketh well to the ways of her household. Put on the whole armour of God. To the Glory of God & in loving memory of

Mary, wife of the Revd John Healy, Archdeacon of Meath, who died Feb. 28 1913, aged 63 years. Also of their son, Guy Bambant Healy, Lieut. Royal Munster Fusiliers, who was killed in action. March 11th 1916. Aged 33 years.' From War Memorial, 1914-1918, Kells Church of Ireland, 'Lieutenant G.R. Healy, Royal Munster Fus. Obituary – Lieut. Guy Rambaut Healy, Kells. From the *Meath Chronicle*, 18 March 1916:

The news of the death of Lieut. Guy Rambaut Healy, son of the Ven. Archdeacon Healy, LL.D., Kells, while taking part in General Smuts' recent engagement at Kitvo, has caused much regret in the district. Lieut. Healy, who was about 33 years of age, served with the Yeomanry Service in the South African War. When the war ended he became attached to the African Game Reserve in which he remained till the outbreak of the present war, when he obtained a transfer from the King's African Rifles, in which regiment he was lieutenant, to the 4th Royal Irish Munster Fusiliers. With the exception of one visit to Ireland, he spent the last twelve years of his life in the colonies. He was killed on the 11th inst., and official intimation of his death was received from the War Office four days later.

HEALY, William: Private, Leinster Regiment, 1st Battalion, D Company. 5210. Born: St Mary's, Meath. Husband of Annie Healy, Beamore Road, Drogheda. Residence: Drogheda. Enlistment location: Drogheda. Killed in action, Egypt, 27 December 1917. Age: 32. Memorial: Y.78, Jerusalem War Cemetery. Drogheda War Memorial.

HEARY, Thomas: Private, Irish Guards, 1st Battalion, 4676. Baptised: Navan, 10 June 1895. Son of Patrick and Margaret Heary, *née* Quigley, Trimgate Street. Father's occupation: Labourer. Occupation: General Labourer. Enlistment location: Drogheda. Killed in action, France & Flanders, 10 January 1915. Memorial: I.A.12, Rue-des-Berceaux Military Cemetery, Richbourg-L'Avoue. From the *Meath Chronicle*, 23 January 1915

Meath and the War – Two Navan Men Killed
Word reached Navan on Tuesday that Joseph Kerrigan, a private in the 1st Leinsters, and Thomas Heary, of Flower Hill, a private in the Irish Guards, had been killed at the front on or about 14th inst. … Private Heary had his head blown off by a shell and his death is deeply mourned in his native town.

HEENEY, Samuel: Private, Royal Dublin Fusiliers, 9th Battalion,

23912. Born: Duleek. Son of Patrick Heeney, Duleek. Residence: Duleek. Enlistment location: Drogheda. Killed in action, France & Flanders, 9 August 1917. Age: 19. Memorial: I.B.12, Potijze Chateau Grounds Cemetery. Drogheda War Memorial.

HENNESSY, Patrick Andrew: Lance-Corporal, Leinster Regiment, 2nd Battalion, 9959. Baptised: Navan 17 January 1898. Son of Patrick and Emily Hennessy, *née* Deare, Flowerhill. Father's occupation: Sergeant, 5th Leinster Regiment. Enlistment location: Dublin. Killed in action, France & Flanders, 31 July 1917. Age: 19. Memorial: Panel 44, Ypres (Menin Gate) Memorial.

HENRY, Michael: Sergeant, Army Service Corps, attached U Anti-Aircraft Battery., M/38532. Baptised St Mary's, Drogheda, 22 September 1885. Son of George and Mary Henry, *née* Madden, Painstown, Colpe West, Drogheda. Father's occupation: Railway Labourer. Husband of late Christine Smyth Henry, Mornington, Drogheda. Enlisted 11 April 1904. Enlistment location: Drogheda. Height: 5 foot 8½ inches. Mobilised Glasgow, 5 August 1914. Died of influenza, France & Flanders, 20 November 1918. Age: 36. Memorial: A.26, Kortijk (St Jan) Communal Cemetery. Award: Military Service Medal.

HIGGINS, Patrick: Private, Royal Irish Fusiliers, 5th Battalion, 17974. Baptised Kells, 8 January 1888. Son of Peter and Bridget Higgins, *née* Rourke, Maudlin Street, Kells. Father's occupation: Shoemaker. Husband of Marie Higgins, 3 Laurel Hurst, College Road, Cork. Residence: Dublin. Enlistment location: Holyhead, Anglesey. Served in Balkans from 7 August 1915. Killed in action, Gallipoli, 10 August 1915. Age: 25. Memorial: Panel 178 to 180, Helles Memorial. From the *Meath Chronicle*, 4 November 1916:

Official news reached his relatives last week of the death of Pte. Patrick Higgins, R.I.F. son of Peter Higgins, Maudlin Street, Kells. He volunteered in February 1915 and left Basingstoke Camp with the 10th Irish Division in June of that year for the Dardanelles. He took part in the landing at Suvla Bay and was reported wounded and missing in an engagement at Chocolate Hill on 10th August 1915. Nothing having been heard of his whereabouts the War Office have intimated that he must be taken as killed in action on that date.

HILL, Edward: Gunner, Royal Garrison Artillery, 27th Siege Battery, 34083. Born: Rathrone, Enfield. Baptised: Rathmolyon parish, 15 February 1891. Son of Michael

Edward Hill.

and Elizabeth Hill, *née* Wiley, Rathrone, Enfield. Father's occupation: Agricultural Labourer. Living: Baconstown, Enfield. Enlistment location: Dublin. Served in France from 5 September 1915. Killed in action, France & Flanders, 27 July 1917. Memorial: XVI.I.9A, Lijssenthoek Military Cemetery. Drogheda War Memorial.

HILL, Patrick: Gunner, Royal Garrison Artillery. 13th Siege Battery. 6456. Baptised: Rathmolyon, 8 August 1880. Son of Michael and Elizabeth Hill, *née* Byrne, Rathrone, Enfield. Enlistment location: Dublin. Served in France from May 1915. Killed in action, France & Flanders, 17 September 1916. Memorial:

I.N.3, Albert Communal Cemetery Extension. Award: Military Medal. Drogheda War Memorial.

HILLEN, Hugh: Private, Royal Irish Fusiliers, 2nd Battalion, 24408. Born: Meath. Brother of Mr James Hillen, 71 Marsh Road, Drogheda. Enlistment location: Drogheda. Died of wounds, France & Flanders, 30 March 1918. Memorial: II.F.4, Adelaide Cemetery, Villers-Bretonneux. Drogheda War Memorial.

HODGINS, Joseph Thomas: Private, 6th Inniskilling Dragoons. 5497. Born: Ardbraccan about 1880. Son of James Barlow and Sarah Hodgins, Faughan Hill Demesne, Martry. Father's occupation: Farmer. Educated: Wilson's Hospital Multyfarnham. Occupation: Saddler. Residence: Killeshandra, Co. Cavan. Died: 29 October 1914. Memorial: Panel 5, Ypres (Menin Gate) Memorial.

HOEY, James: Trimmer, Mercantile Marine, SS *Lusitania*, Liverpool. Baptised: Duleek, 15 May 1891. Son of John and Rose Hoey, *née* Conlon, Garballagh, Duleek. Drowned as a result of an enemy submarine attack, 7 May 1915. Age: 23. Memorial: Tower Hill Memorial.

HOLDEN, Sidney Naldrett: Private, Royal Warwickshire Regiment, 14th Battalion, 693.

Baptised Navan, 2 December 1894. Son of Allen George Naldrett and Jane Sophia Holden, Brewshill and later of 46 Park Road, Sparkhill, Birmingham. Father's occupation: Drum Major. Residence: Sparkhill, Birmingham. Enlistment location: Birmingham. Served in France from 21 November 1915. Killed in action, France & Flanders, 31 August 1916. Age: 21. Memorial: V.A.7, Flatiron Copse Cemetery, Mametz.

HOLMES, Oliver Wendall: Second Lieutenant, Royal Inniskilling Fusiliers, 7th Battalion. Baptised Trim, 6 September 1896. Son of Michael and Mary Anne Holmes, Trim. Father's occupation: Head Constable, RIC. Father later lived at Georgeville, Balbriggan, Co. Dublin. Served in France from 17 December 1915. Died of wounds in German hands, 16 August 1917. Memorial: Panel 70 to 72, Tyne Cot Memorial. '2nd Lieutenant O.W. Holmes, Royal Inniskilling Fus' (War Memorial, 1914-1918, Kells Church of Ireland). From the *Meath Chronicle*, 13 April 1918:

> The War Office has sent District Inspector Holmes, Kells, official news that his eldest son, 2nd Lieut. O.W. Holmes who had been missing since the 18th August last, has been "presumed" killed on that date. His only other son, S.B. Holmes, has joined the Indian Army and intelligence of his

safe arrival in India has just been received.

HOPKINS, James: Private, Royal Dublin Fusiliers, 8/9th Battalion, 14611. Born: Kells. Enlistment location: Dublin. Served in France from 20 December 1915. Killed in action, France & Flanders, 25 December 1917. Memorial: II.G.21, Unicorn Cemetery, Vend'Huile.

HORAN, William: Private, Irish Guards, 2nd Battalion, 6924. Baptised: Oristown, 3 May 1890. Son of William and Mary Horan, née Clarke, Horan's Cross, Fyanstown, Kells. Father's occupation: Agricultural Labourer. Occupation: Labourer. Enlistment location: Drogheda. Served in France from 17 August 1915. Killed in action, France & Flanders, 2 July 1916. Age: 26. Memorial: Panel 11, Ypres (Menin Gate) Memorial.

HUGHES, Bernard: Private, Irish Guards, 1st Battalion, 4376. Baptised: Beauparc, 22 March 1889. Son of Thomas and Mary Hughes, née Connor, Kentstown and later at Brownstown and Skryne. Father's occupation: Tailor. Occupation: Tailor. Enlistment location: Dublin. Served in France from 13 August 1914. Died of wounds, France & Flanders, 29 April 1915. Died a prisoner of war in Germany. Memorial: III. K. 3, Niederzwehren Cemetery.

HUSSEY, Patrick: Private, Leinster Regiment, 2nd Battalion, 3600. Born: Longwood. Enlistment location: Edenderry. Served in France from 25 October 1914. Killed in action, Loos, France, 10 January 1917. Age: 26. Memorial: Panel 127, Loos Memorial.

I

IRVINE, William: Lance-Corporal, Royal Inniskilling Fusiliers, 9th Battalion, 17868. Born: Fermanagh. Son of John and Anne Irvine, Lankill, Culkey PO, Enniskillen, Co. Fermanagh. Father's occupation: (1898) Coachman, (1911) Caretaker and Herd. Residence: Allenstown, Kells. Occupation: Groom and Domestic Servant. Enlistment location: Enniskillen. Served in France from 5 October 1915. Killed in action, France & Flanders, 29 March 1918. Memorial: Panel 38 to 40, Pozieres Memorial.

IRWIN, Thomas: Private, Irish Guards, 2nd Battalion, 5595. Born: Kells. Son of Thomas and Kate Irwin, Cross Street, Kells. Father's occupation: Agricultural Labourer. Husband of Bridget Irwin. Enlistment location: Navan. Killed in action, France & Flanders, 3 August 1917. Age: 21. Memorial: X.E.19, Artillery Wood Cemetery.

J

JAMES, W.: Private, Wiltshire Regiment. Killed, France, 1915. From the *Meath Chronicle*, 27 May 1915, 'A heavy toll of killed, wounded and missing has resulted from the recent fighting in Flanders. The casualty list contains the following names – Pte W. James, Dowdstown of the Wiltshire Regt.'

JAMESON, Edward John: Lieutenant Colonel, Leinster Regiment, 5th Battalion, attached to Essex Regiment, 4th Battalion. Son of John William and Alice Rose Grace Jameson, Delvin Lodge. Previously served in the 14th Hussars and on retiring prior to the Great War joined the Reserve of Officers. Died of wounds, 27 March 1917. Age: 42. Award: DSO. Memorial: C.83, Deir El Belah War Cemetery, Israel. Julianstown church, stained-glass window 'Edward J. Jameson Lt. Colonel Leinster Regiment killed in action in Palestine 27th March 1917'.

JENKIN, Victor David: Private, Royal Dublin Fusiliers, 3rd Battalion, 19879. Born: Glamorganshire. Son of Noah and Mary Ann Jenkin. Occupation: (1911) Footman, Headfort House, Kells. Residence: Wenvoe, Glamorganshire. Enlistment location: Dublin. Served in Balkans in 1915. Died at home, 28 October 1918. Age: 32. Memorial: 1.1, Wenvoe (St Mary) Churchyard Extension.

JENKINS, William: Rifleman, Royal Irish Rifles, 18th Battalion, 1139. Born: Ardbraccan. Son of Robert and Marie Jenkins, Ardbraccan, Navan. Father's occupation: Garden Labourer. Died at home, 19 January 1916. Age: 24. Memorial: Screen Wall, H.534, Belfast City Cemetery. From Roll of Honour, Ardbraccan church, now in St Mary's church Navan, 'William Jenkins, aged 25 years, Royal Irish Rifles died Purdysburn Hospital 19 Jan 1916.'

JENNINGS, Fred: Private, Royal Irish Regiment. War Memorial, 1914-1918, Kells Church of Ireland and Roll of Honour, St Mary's church, Navan. His connection to Meath is unclear as there are no records of an F. Jennings. Suggested person is Fred Jennings, Lance-Corporal, Royal Irish Rifles, 1st Battalion, 1345. Son of Jane Jennings of Ruston, Wykeham, York. Died: 1 July 1916. Age: 19. Memorial: Pier and Face 15AS and 15B Thiepval Memorial.

K

KANE, Patrick: (alias Francis Keane) Private, Leinster Regiment, 6th Battalion, 114. Secondary Regiment: Labour Corps, 119546. Died of wounds, Co. Meath Infirmary, Navan, 3 March 1919. Memorial: Athlumney Old Graveyard.

KEALY, William: Private, Connaught Rangers, 1st Battalion, 10933. Born: 6 November 1890, Trim. Residence: Navan. Brother, James, Trimgate Street, Navan. Sister, Mary J. Enlisted 2 May 1914. Enlistment location: Dublin. Age at enlistment: 23. Occupation: Tram Conductor. Height: 5 foot 5½ inches. Complexion: Fresh. Eyes: Grey. Hair: Black. Served in France from 7 October 1914. Killed in action at Mauser Ridge, north of Ypres, when the Connaught Rangers were involved in a huge counter attack during the 2nd Battle of Ypres. Most of the Rangers who died in this battle were gassed. Killed in action, France & Flanders, 26 April 1915. His sister Mary J. Kealy wrote a number of times to seek information from the military authorities as she had got 'no news from him for a very long time and was most anxious about him. (October 1915).' Not married. Memorial: Panel 42, Ypres (Menin Gate) Memorial.

KEANE, Francis: *see* **KANE, Patrick.**

KEAPPOCK, John Alfred: Royal Navy, HMS *Shark*, Engine Room Artificer 4th Class. M/4997. Son of Joseph and Catherine Keappock, Claremount, Navan. Father's occupation: Merchant. Drowned off Jutland following a battle in the North Sea, 31 May 1916. Age: 26. Memorial: 15, Portsmouth Naval Memorial. From the *Meath Chronicle*, 10 June 1916:

> Navan Bluejacket Missing
> On Monday last Mr. Joseph Keappock U.D.C. Navan, received notification that his second eldest son, John, who was a second hand artificer on board the "Shark," was missing. Since then the list of survivors from this vessel has been published, but his name does not appear in it. Although official notification of his death has not been received it is feared that his chances of having been saved are remote. When about 23 he joined HMS "Harrier" on which he remained about six months and was then transferred to the "Shark" on which he spent the last two years.

From the *Meath Chronicle*, 17 June 1916:

Navan Man Lost in North Sea Fight

Last week Mr. John Keappock, employed as engineer on the HMS Shark, sunk in the North Sea battle, was reported as missing. We regret to say that the worst fears of his friends have been realised. His father, Mr. Joseph Keappock, U.D.C., has received a communication from the Admirality intimating their belief that the gallant young fellow had been numbered among the victims of what has been described as the greatest sea fight in the world's history. Mr. Keappock was considered exceptionally clever at his work and had every prospect of a distinguished career in the navy. Of a manly and chivalrous character, he was a prime favourite amongst his comrades. The fact that he was engaged to be married adds a pathetic feature to the sadness of his untimely death which is mourned by many friends.

KEELAN, Joseph: Private, Irish Guards, 2ⁿᵈ Battalion, 11545. Born: Meath Hill. Baptised: Drumconrath, 24 December 1892. Son of Christopher and Anne Keelan, *née* Carolan, Ballyhoe. Father's occupation: Farmer. Residence: Ballyhoe, Co. Meath. Enlistment location: Dublin. Killed in action, France & Flanders, 28 March 1918. Memorial: Bay 1, Arras Memorial.

KELLETT, Thomas: Corporal, Royal Irish Fusiliers, 7ᵗʰ Battalion, 17446. Baptised Kilskyre/Ballinlough, 19 November 1897. Son of Thomas and Anne Kellett, *née* Gilsenan, Seymourstown. Father's occupation: Farmer. Enlistment location: Cavan. Served in France from 23 March 1915. Died of wounds, France & Flanders, 22 August 1916. Age: 18. Memorial: Sp. Mem. 21, Bois-Carre Military Cemetery, Haisnes.

KELLY, Joseph: Private, Royal Irish Fusiliers, 1ˢᵗ Battalion, 6625. Born: Navan. Residence: Wilkinstown. Enlistment location: Drogheda. Died of wounds, France & Flanders, 18 October 1914. Memorial: IX.A.92, Cite Bonjean Military Cemetery, Armentieres.

KENEALLY, Charles: Private, Irish Guards, 1ˢᵗ Battalion, 1130. Baptised Julianstown, 20 August 1875. Son of Mathew and Maria Keneally, Laytown. Father's occupation: Coastguard. Enlistment location: Glasgow. Served in France from 23 November 1914. Killed in action, France & Flanders, 30 December 1914. Memorial: I.D.15, Le Touret Military Cemetery, Richebourg-L'Avoue. Drogheda War Memorial.

KENNEDY, Peter: Private, Leinster Regiment. 7985. Skryne. Died of wounds. From the *Meath Chronicle*, 5 December 1914:

Meathmen Killed and Wounded News has reached Skryne that Peter Kennedy, of the Leinsters, has been killed in action in France. He was instructor to the Skryne Volunteers before the war broke out. He was an able instructor, and his sad death is deeply felt by the members of the Skryne Corps.

KENNEDY, Thomas: Sergeant, Leinster Regiment, 6th Battalion, 271. Born: Oristown. Uncle of Maryanne Kennedy, Teltown View, Navan. Enlistment location: Navan. Served in Balkans from 5 August 1915. Killed in action, Gallipoli, 11 August 1915. Memorial: Sp. Mem. B. 81, Embarkation Pier Cemetery. Drogheda War Memorial. From the *Meath Chronicle*, 11 September 1915:

Deep regret has been occasioned in Oristown district by the news that Sergt. Thomas Kennedy, drill instructor to the local Volunteer corps, has been killed at the Dardanelles. The deceased, who belonged to the Royal Garrison Artillery, was brother to Mr. Richard Kennedy, waterworks overseer, Kells, with whom many friends sympathise.

From the *Meath Chronicle*, 18 September 1915:

Volunteer Drill Instructor Killed. During the week Capt. Collins of Gibbstown Castle, received news that Sergt. Thomas Kennedy of Donaghpatrick, had been killed in action at Suvla Bay. The deceased, who was brother to Mr. Richard Kennedy, waterworks overseer, Kells, with whom many friends sympathise enlisted in the Royal Garrison Artillery and was on his way to the South African War when peace was proclaimed. On leaving the army as a reservist, Sergt. Kennedy returned home, and when the Volunteer movement was started he was appointed drill instructor to the Oristown and Kilbarry corps, a post for which his military training well fitted him, and in which he earned the confidence and esteem of the members of the corps, who have heard with deep regret of his sad fate. On the outbreak of war he re-joined his old regiment, but was transferred to the 5th Leinsters with whom he went to the front. Soon after landing he was slightly wounded and recovering rapidly, went back to the firing line, being killed about August 14th.

KENNY, William: Dublin Fusiliers, O'Growney Terrace, Navan. From the *Meath Chronicle*, 28 November 1914, 'Meathmen Killed and Wounded. Mr. Gilliatt of Archall and Private Wm. Kenny, O'Growney Terrace, Navan of the Dublin Fusiliers, are also reported to have been killed.'

KENNY, Thomas: Stoker, Royal Naval Reserve, HMS *Hampshire*, 7200s. Baptised: Slane, 24 August 1875. Son of Peter and Cecilia Kenny, *née* Walsh, Slane and later of Hinchey's Lane, Drogheda. Occupation: (1901) Agricultural Labourer, (1911) Labourer, Chemical Works. Husband of Mary Anne Kenny, *née* Munster, Plattin Road, Drogheda. Killed in mine explosion off Orkneys, 5 June 1916. Age: 41. Memorial: 23, Portsmouth Naval Memorial. Drogheda War Memorial.

KERRIGAN, Joseph: Lance-Corporal, Leinster Regiment, 1st Battalion, 9297. Baptised: Navan, 12 September 1889. Son of Joseph and Kate Kerrigan, *née* McCluskey, Railway Street, Navan. Mother's occupation: Midwifery nurse. Enlistment location: Navan. Served in France from 19 December 1914. Killed in action on Wednesday, 13 January 1915, St Eloi, Flanders. Age 25. Memorial: Panel 44, Ypres (Menin Gate) Memorial. From the *Meath Chronicle*, 23 January 1915:

Meath and the War – Two Navan Men Killed
Word reached Navan on Tuesday that Joseph Kerrigan, a private in the 1st Leinsters, and Thomas Heary, of Flower Hill, a private in the Irish Guards, had been killed at the front on or about 14th inst. Private Kerrigan, who served

some time in India before the war, was a well-known and popular member of the Navan Harps, and was one of their best players. His brother, Thomas, who is serving in the same regiment was present at the interment. The sad news was learned with deep regret in Navan where heartfelt sympathy with his widowed mother, who recently received a letter from the King complimenting her on having five sons in the army. On the day the sad news was received some friends of the deceased posted scapulars for him. Pte. Kerrigan, it was stated, was shot through the head.

KIERAN, James: Private, Leinster Regiment, 2nd Battalion, 4899. Born: Castletown. Enlistment location: Drogheda. Died of wounds, France & Flanders, 31 March 1916. Memorial: II.B.53, Bailleul Communal Cemetery Extension (Nord).

KIERNAN, Patrick: Private, Royal Dublin Fusiliers, 2nd Battalion, 18379. Born: Oldcastle. Enlistment location: Coatsbridge. Served in France from 27 May 1915. Killed in action, France & Flanders, 8 August 1915. Memorial: III.A.2, Sucerie Military Cemetery, Colincamps.

KIERNAN, James Leo: Private, South Wales Borders, 5th Battalion, 41565. Baptised: Oldcastle, 11 April

1899. Son of Peter and Margaret Kiernan, *née* Walsh, Oldcastle and later of 33 Chacery Street, Wigan. Residence: Wigan. Enlistment location: Ashton-Under-Lyne. Killed in action, France & Flanders, 7 June 1918. Age: 19. Memorial: VI.F.4, Marfaux British Cemetery.

KILLEEN, Michael: Private, Royal Dublin Fusiliers, 2ⁿᵈ Battalion, 20230. Born: Longwood. Son of John and Mary Killeen, Longwood. Husband of Jane Killeen, 33 Constitution Hill, Dublin. Occupation: Coal Labourer. Enlistment location: Dublin. Served in France from 14 December 1915. Killed in action, France & Flanders, 23 October 1916. Age: 39. Memorial: Pier and Face 16 C, Thiepval Memorial.

KING, Lawrence: Seaman, Royal Naval Reserve, HMS *Bulwark*. 5810A. Born: Mornington. Baptised St Mary's, Drogheda, 18 January 1891. Son of John and Margaret King, *née* Garvey, Mornington, Drogheda. Father's occupation: Farmer. Joined the Navy at the outbreak of the war and was lost on the explosion of the HMS *Bulwark*. Killed 26 November 1914. Memorial: 6, Portsmouth Naval Memorial. Drogheda War Memorial.

KINEALLY, James: Private, Australian Army (Trim Church of Ireland, Roll of Honour).

L

LANCASTER, Charles Edward Archibald: Corporal, Royal Canadian Dragoons, 114340. Born: Co. Meath, 30 June 1893. Son of Dr William Cooke and Jane Brabazon Moore Lancaster, *née* Lugton, Arranmore, Hill of Down, Co. Meath. Brother, Thomas, also killed in the war. Father's occupation: Doctor. Educated Morgan's School, Dublin, 1904-10. Occupation: Farmer. Enlisted 28 December 1914. Enlistment location: North Bomford, Canada. Height: 5 foot 8 inches. Complexion: Dark. Eyes: Brown. Hair: Dark Brown. Killed in action, 30 March 1918. Age: 25. Memorial: Vimy Memorial.

LANCASTER, Thomas Arthur Victor: Lance-Corporal, Royal Montreal Regiment, Machine Gun Corps, 14th Battalion, 919962. Born: Co. Westmeath, 5 May 1897. Son of Dr William Cooke and Jane Brabazon Moore Lancaster, *née* Lugton, Arranmore, Hill of Down, Co. Meath. His brother Charles, also killed in the war. Father's occupation: Doctor. Educated Morgan's School, Dublin. Residence: Isaleigh, Grange, Danville, Canada. Occupation: Farm Labourer. Enlisted 18 September 1916. Enlistment location: Montreal, Canada. Complexion: Fair. Eyes: Brown. Hair: Dark Brown. Killed in action, 2 September 1918.

Memorial: I.F.9, Dominion Cemetery, Hendecourt-Les-Cagnicourt.

LANE, Charles Willington Tremayne: Major, 7th Dragoon Guards (Princess Royal's). Born: Bellary, Madras, India, 15 September 1888. Son of Col. Samuel Willington Lane, Rathkenny. Educated: Royal Military College, Sandhurst. Gazetted Second Lieutenant 7th Dragoon Guards, January 1908. Died of wounds, 4 April 1918. Memorial: I.G.8, Namps-Au-Val British Cemetery. Awards: Military Cross.

LANE, James: Served as Clarke. Sergeant, Royal Irish Regiment, 7th Battalion, 2066. Born: Slane. Son of John and Mary Lane. Husband of Mrs E. Lane, Mooretown, Slane. Killed in action, France & Flanders, 19 September 1918. Age: 32. Award: Military Medal. Memorial: Panels 51 to 52, Tyne Cot Memorial. Drogheda War Memorial.

LANGAN, Eugene: Gunner, Royal Field Artillery, C Batttery. 283rd Brigade, 101180. Born: 7 March 1896, Co. Kildare. Son of John and Mary Langan, *née* Redmond, Weston, Duleek. Father's occupation: Coachman. Brother, James, also killed in war. Educated: Maynooth National School. Enlisted: 6 October

1915. Enlistment location: Athlone. Died of wounds, France & Flanders, 20 September 1916. Age: 20. Not married. Memorial: II.C.39, Bronfay Farm Military Cemetery, Bray-sur-Somme.

LANGAN, James: Corporal, Royal Berkshire Regiment, 5th Battalion, 10386. Born: Enfield, 12 November 1889. Eldest son of John and Mary Langan, *née* Redmond, Weston, Duleek. Father's occupation: Coachman. Brother, Eugene, also killed in war. Educated: Maynooth National School. Served his apprenticeship in the racing stables. Residence: Duleek. Enlisted on the outbreak of war 17 August 1914. Enlistment location: Reading. Served in France from March 1915. Wounded he was killed by a shell, while assisting the doctor to bandage a wounded comrade, both of whom were killed by the same shell. His comrades erected a cross with his name. Killed in action, Loos, France, 13 October 1915. Age: 26. Not married. Memorial: Panel 93 to 95, Loos Memorial.

LAUGHRAN: C.R.F.A. (Trim Church of Ireland, Roll of Honour).

LEDDY, Patrick: Served as Dolan. Private, South Lancashire Regiment, 2nd Battalion, 7826. Baptised: Kells, 15 August 1881. Son of Patrick and Mary Leddy, *née* Byrne, Pitcher Lane, Kells. Father's occupation: Agricultural Labourer. His brother, Peter, killed in action. His brother, Michael, was wounded and rendered unfit for service. Enlistment location: Dublin. Served in France from 14 August 1914. Killed in action, France & Flanders, 24 October 1914. Age: 30. Memorial: Panel 23, Le Touret Memorial.

LEDDY, Peter: Private, Leinster Regiment, 2nd Battalion, 3207. Baptised: Kells, 17 June 1877. Son of Patrick and Mary Leddy, *née* Byrne, Pitcher Lane, Kells. Father's occupation: Agricultural Labourer. His brother, Patrick, killed in action. His brother, Michael, was wounded and rendered unfit for service. Enlistment location: Mosney. Served in France from 2 April 1915. Killed in action, France & Flanders, 27 April 1916. Memorial: II.C.9, Ration Farm (La Plus Douve) Annexe. From the *Meath Chronicle*, 13 May 1916:

Kells Soldier Killed at the Front. We regret to learn that intimation has been received that Private Peter Leddy, Fair Green, Kells of the Leinster Regiment, has been killed in action in France. The deceased who was a respectable young man re-joined the army at the outbreak of the war as a reservist, and with the exception of one or two brief periods of leave, had been at the front since. He has a brother at the front, while his younger brother, Michael Leddy, was wounded in the arm and rendered unfit for service. With poor Leddy's aged mother and family warm sympathy is felt.

LEDWIDGE, Francis Edward: Lance-Corporal, Royal Inniskilling Fusiliers, 1st Battalion, 16138. Born: 19 August 1887. Son of Patrick and Anne Ledwidge, *née* Lynch, Slane. Enlistment location: Navan. A prolific poet noted for his pastoral pieces about Meath; his last poems made subtle reference to war. Killed in action, France & Flanders, 31 July 1917. Age: 29. Memorial: II.B.5, Artillery Wood Cemetery. Drogheda War Memorial. From the *Meath Chronicle*, 13 May 1916:

Meath Poet-Soldier Among the Servians [*sic*]
Mr. Francis Ledwidge, the gifted Meath poet, who joined the Inniskilling Fusiliers, and who has been on active service for the past year, and at present home on leave, speaking to our representative, remarked: "The Servians impressed me very much. I consider Servia, poetically like Ireland – a poor old woman wandering the roads of the world." In the course of further conversation he stated that they found strips of cloth in some of the Servian houses bearing in faded letters the word "welcome". Those cloths had been hung across the streets. "While in the Dardanelles" he said, with a smile, "we were not short of cigarettes. The Turks exchanged cigarettes with us for beef and biscuits. If I give you any more information I'll have nothing left for the book I am going to write about my experiences out here.

From the *Meath Chronicle*, 11 August 1917:

Death of Slane Poet
Francis E. Ledwidge Killed at the Front
It is with regret we record the death of Francis Ledwidge, the peasant poet of Meath, who was killed in Flanders on the 31st July. His passing removes one whom Lord Dunsany in a graceful tribute to his memory says: "Ireland would have lawfully claimed, as she may yet, the greatest of peasant singers." He was born in 1892 in Slane, where he lived the greater part of his brief life and about which he wrote the majority of his poems. He was a poet of nature. The blackbirds and arboured lanes of his native village formed themes for poems which astonished many who read them by their "freshess and their beauty". His description of the blackbird, written at the age of sixteen would certainly pass for the work of a more mature and cultured mind than one could hope for in an Irish peasant boy.

And wonderous impudently sweet
Half of him passion, half conceit,
The blackbird calls down the street
Like a piper of Hamlin.

"Roses will bloom in lanes in Meath," says Lord Dunsany, "for thousands of years to come and blackbirds will charm other hearts, and the Boyne still sweep to the sea, and others may love these things as much as Ledwidge loved them but they were all so much pictured upon his heart and he sang so gladly of them, that something is lost which those fields would have given up and may never give again."

During all his time he was at the Front he wrote, and always of his native place. No matter where he found himself, whether in France or Egypt, Flanders or Gallipoli, his poetic dreams were ever guided home to his beloved Meath. His last volume, "Songs of Peace" contains most of these poems, but many remain yet in manuscript. In one of his last songs, written in Belgium, dated July 1917, he seemed to foreshadow his approaching doom.

On this edge of life I seem to hover,
For I knew my love had come at last;
That my joy was past and gladness over.
May he rest in peace.

LEGGE-BOURKE, Nigel Walter Henry: Lieutenant, Coldstream Guards, 2nd Battalion. Born: Grosvenor Square, London, 13 November 1889. Son of Colonel the Hon. Sir Harry Legge, KCVO of Hayes, Navan, and the Hon. Lady Amy Gwendoline, Maid to Queen Victoria 1877-84, daughter of Gustavus William Lambart of Beauparc. Educated Evelyns, Mr G.T. Worsley's, Eton and the Royal Military College, Sandhurst. Gazetted Second Lieutenant, Coldstream Guards, 6 February 1900 and promoted Lieutenant 6 June 1910. Served with the Expeditionary Force France from 12 August 1914. Married to Lady Victoria Carrington, youngest daughter of the first Marquess of Lincolnshire, K.G. 3 June 1913 at the Guards Chapel, Wellington Barracks. Son, Edward Alexander Henry, born 16 May 1914. Killed in action, near Ypres, 30 October 1914, while in command of a platoon of No. 1 Coy. holding advanced trenches in Rental Wood. Age: 24. Memorial: Panel 11, Ypres (Menin Gate) Memorial. From the *Meath Chronicle*, 21 November 1914:

> Sportsmen Killed in the War
> That the Meath Hunt is suffering its own share as a result of the war is further exemplified by the sad news that several of its prominent followers have been killed while in action. Among the list of the dead published recently are Capt.

F. Browning, R.F.A, Dundalk, Capt Ford, Hon. W.R. Wyndham, 17th Lancers; Lieutenant Matheson, K.R.F.Tara Hall; F.H.B. Blaithwayt, 2nd Life Guards; Lieut. Ballayxe, 11th Hussars; Lionel H. Partry, 5th Dragoon Guards; and Lieut. Legge Burke, Coldstream Guards, Hayes, Beauparc, nephew and successor to the late Hon. Harry Burke.

The deceased officers, some used to stay at the Club, Navan were ardent and popular followers of the Meaths, and are deeply regretted by all who knew them.

LEITCH, Neil: Corporal, Argyll and Sutherland Highlanders, 8th Battalion, 301439. Son of Alexander and Margaret Leitch, 45 Union Street, Lochgilphead, Argyllshire. In 1911 recorded as Agricultural Instructor, aged 30, living with James and Mary Clark at Robinrath, Navan. Enlistment location: Rothesay, Butes. Killed in action, 7 September 1917. Age: 29. Memorial II.B.7, Gwalia Cemetery. Roll of Honour, St Mary's church, Navan.

LEONARD, John: Private, Royal Dublin Fusiliers, 8th Battalion, 23930. Baptised: Donore, 17 August 1888. Son of Patrick and Jane Leonard, née Reilly, Donore. Residence: Donore. Enlistment location: Drogheda. Enlisted: 9 October 1915. Age at enlistment: 28. Occupation: Labourer. Height: 5 foot 4 inches. Complexion:

Fresh. Hair: Fair. Eyes: Grey. Served in France from 29 March 1916. Gassed 29 April 1916. Died of wounds, France & Flanders, 22 May 1916. Memorial: I.J.8, Chocques Military Cemetery. Drogheda War Memorial.

LEONARD, Michael Joseph: Rifleman. Royal Inniskilling Fusiliers 1st Battalion, 9838. Baptised: Navan, 21 October 1889. Son of Christopher and Julia Leonard, née Caffrey, Graigs, Navan and later of 22 Hendrick Street, Dublin. Father's occupation (1911): Wagon fitter. Raised in Trim and became a shoemaker and mender. Residence: Dublin. Died of phthisis, 1 May 1915. Age: 25. Buried in Trimulgherry Cantonment Cemetery. Memorial: Face 14, Madras 1914-1918 War Memorial, Chennai.

LEONARD, Patrick: Lance-Corporal, Machine Gun Corps (Infantry), 52511. Formerly 5th Lancers, 4840. Born: Shoeburyness, Essex. Son of James and Mary Leonard, Dunboyne. Father's occupation: Rural Postman. Occupation: Rural Auxiliary Postman. Husband of Margaret Leonard, Bennetstown, Dunboyne. Children: Patrick and James: Residence: Dunboyne. Enlistment location: Dublin. Killed in action: France & Flanders, 24 October 1918. Age: 30. Memorial: C.17, Ingoyghem Military Cemetery. Letter from Commanding Officer:

Patrick Leonard.

3/12/18
No. 5 Hut MGC
No. 17 Company
"B" Camp
Alnwick
Northumberland
My dear Mrs Leonard,

I cannot find words to express as I would wish the sorrow I feel for you in your irreparable loss by the death of poor Paddy. Accept my most heartfelt sympathy. Just when his hopes were brightened he was called away from you and all who loved him. Never had I a pal "out yonder" like poor Paddy and to my dying day I can never forget him and all he was to me in those awful days of trial and fighting.

Do not grieve Mrs Leonard for although Paddy is not with us on earth yet I firmly believe we shall all be reunited in the next world. What a glorious death! No man could die better. I can almost see poor Paddy's manly handsome and cheerful face again as if it had only been yesterday. He was one of the most fearless men I have ever met and was always the cheeriest and braves in our section "out there".

I feel as if I had lost a brother. We were kindred souls and were never separated when once we met until fate sent me across to Blighty. Oh how I wished that Paddy had come with me, but it was not to be. God's will must always prevail. Now I think I have said enough,

28/10/18
Dear Mrs Leonard,

I am writing to try to express the sympathy of myself and section to you in your great trouble. Perhaps you may find some consolation in the fact that your husband was killed instantly and suffered no pain.

I have been his section officer for some time and can truthfully say that we have lost one of our best men in the Company. He was always cheery and willing and a great example to his comrades.

I am

Yours sincerely

L. Exshaw 2/Lt

so once again I tender my heart-felt sympathy to you and to the kiddies. I loved Paddy almost as a brother and I would love to be of some little aid to those he loved. Let me know if there is any little thing I might do to help you bear your burden.

In deep sorrow,

I remain

Most sincerely yours

Ernest A. Hewardine

P.S. If it is not too much to ask you Mrs Leonard could you send me a photo of Paddy. He promised me one but I never got it. Does not matter if it's only a snap I shall get it enlarged and treasure it ever. Write to c/o 49 Moyne Road, Rathmines, Dublin as I may be leaving here soon. E.A.H.

(Letters and photograph courtesy of Councillor Noel Leonard, Patrick Leonard's nephew).

LONERGAN, Daniel: Private, Irish Guards, 1st Battalion, 11603. Baptised: St Mary's Drogheda, 2 February 1890. Son of Edmund and Annie Lonergan, *née* Keegan, Old Hill, Drogheda and later of Cullindragh, Culmullin. Father's occupation: (1901) Ex-Sergeant RIC, (1911) Farmer. Brother, John Francis, also killed in the war. Killed in action, France & Flanders, 27 August 1918 Age: 28. Memorial Reference: Panel 3, Vis-en-Artois Memorial.

LONERGAN, John Francis: Private, Irish Guards, 2nd Battalion, 10682. Born: Co. Louth. Son of Edmund and Annie Lonergan, *née* Keegan, Old Hill, Drogheda and later of Cullindragh, Culmullin. Father's occupation: (1901) Ex-Sergeant RIC, (1911) Farmer. Brother, Daniel, also killed in the war. Enlistment location: Grays, Essex. Died of wounds, France & Flanders, 2 August 1917. Age: 22. Memorial: II.I.1, Dozinghem Military Cemetery.

LOWNDES, Thomas: Private, Irish Guards, 1st Battalion, 9714. Baptised Oldcastle, 30 May 1891. Son of George and Rose Lowdnes, *née* Lynch, Milltown. Father's occupation: Shoemaker. Occupation: General Labourer. Died of wounds, France & Flanders, 24 September 1916. Age: 28. Memorial: II.C.57, Dartmoor Cemetery, Becordel-Becourt.

LOWRY, Joseph Ewart: Temporary Lieutenant, Royal Irish Regiment, 2nd Battalion. Baptised: Ardbraccan, 19 May 1898. Son of Albert John and Emma Olivia Lowry, Oatlands, Durhamstown and later of Bachelors Lodge, Navan. Father's occupation: Gentleman Farmer. Killed in action, 25 August 1918. Age: 20. Memorial: II.I.18, Adanac Military Cemetery, Miraumont. From Roll of Honour Ardbraccan church now in St Mary's church, Navan, 'Joseph Edward Lowry aged 20 years. 2nd Lieut Royal Irish Regiment killed in action at Bapaume 25 August 1918.'

LYNAGH, Patrick: Stoker, Royal Naval Reserve, HMS *Vanguard*, 5831s. Baptised: Slane, 18 April 1886. Son of John and Elizabeth Lynagh, *née* Dunegan, Harlenstown, Slane. Father's occupation: Farmer. Occupation: Farmer's son. Served at the Battle of Jutland. Killed by internal explosion of vessel at Scapa Flow, 9 July 1917. Memorial: 28, Portsmouth Naval Memorial.

LYNCH, Charles Joseph: Corporal, Royal Dublin Fusiliers, 2nd Battalion, 6707. Baptised: Slane, 23 December 1880. Son of James and Bridget Lynch, *née* Duff, Fennor House, Slane. Residence: Slane. Enlisted: 25 August 1899. Enlistment location: Curragh Camps. Occupation: Electrician. Age at enlistment: 18 years. Served in the 4th Dublin Fusiliers Militia. Height: 5 foot 8 inches. Complexion: Sallow. Eyes: Grey. Hair: Dark Brown. Served in South Africa campaign. Served in France from 13 August 1914. Killed in action, France & Flanders, 20 November 1914. Age: 33. Memorial: Panel 10, Ploegsteert Memorial. Drogheda War Memorial.

LYNCH, John: Private. Irish Guards, 1st Batt, No. 1 Company, 3304. Born: Kilmessan. Son of Philip and Kate Lynch, Main Street, Clonmellon, Co. Westmeath. Served in France from 13 August 1914. Killed in action, France & Flanders, 6 November 1914. Age: 24. Memorial: Panel 11, Ypres (Menin Gate) Memorial.

LYNCH, Patrick: Private, Irish Guards, 1st Battalion, 4458. Born: Mitchelstown. Baptised: Athboy, 23 February 1893. Son of Mark and Elizabeth Lynch, *née* Ward, Mitchelstown, Athboy. Occupation: Groom, Domestic Servant. Enlistment location: Dublin. Served in France from 13 August 1914. Killed in action, France & Flanders, 6 November 1914. Age: 22. Memorial: Panel 11, Ypres (Menin Gate) Memorial.

LYNCH, Patrick: Pioneer, Royal Engineers, WR/341152. Baptised: Carnaross, 28 September 1868. Son of Peter and Mary Lynch, *née* Farrelly, Carnaross. Father's occupation: Farmer. Husband of Rose Lynch, 59 Lower Dominick Street, Dublin. Four children in 1911 census. Occupation: Carter's Labourer. Died: 6 May 1918. Memorial: 25.RC.51, Newport (St Woolos) Cemetery.

LYONS, Christopher: Private, Royal Dublin Fusiliers, C Company. 7th Battalion, attached 1st Battalion, 15999. Baptised Bohermeen, 5 April 1896. Son of John and Anne Lyons, *née* Donaghy, Ardbraccan, Navan. Father's occupation: Tailor. Occupation: (1911) Tailor's Apprentice. Died: France & Flanders, 2 March 1919. Age: 22. Memorial: B.19, Kortrijk (St Jan.) Communal Cemetery.

LYSTER, John Lyster: R.N. (First World War Memorial, St Kieran's church Loughcrew.)

M

McCABE, Andrew: Private, Leinster Regiment, 6th Battalion, 4397. Baptised: Kells, 18 May 1882. Son of Andrew and Rose McCabe, *née* Madden, Church View, Kells. Father's occupation: Labourer. Occupation: (1901) Labourer, (1911) Jarvey. Married about 1905. Husband of Mary Anne McCabe, Church Lane, Kells and later 19 St Patrick's Terrace, Navan. Father to Mary Rose. Residence: Navan. Enlistment location: Navan. Served in France. Died of wounds, Salonica, 11 May 1917. Memorial: IX.C.8, Struma Military Cemetery, Kalocastron, Greece.

McCANN, Cornelius: Private, Connaught Rangers, 2nd Battalion, 8202. Born: Nobber. Residence: Dublin. Enlistment location: Dublin. Served in France from 14 August 1914. Killed in action, France & Flanders, 12 November 1914. Memorial: Panel 42, Ypres (Menin Gate) Memorial.

McCANN, Joseph: Private, Royal Irish Fusiliers, 5th Battalion, 18211. Baptised St Mary's, Drogheda 10 February 1894. Son of James and Bridget McCann, *née* Berrill, West Colpe, Drogheda. Enlistment location: Drogheda. Killed in action, Gallipoli, 16 August 1915. Age: 21. Memorial: Panel 178 to 180, Helles Memorial.

McCANN, Joseph: Private, Irish Guards, 2nd Battalion, 8956. Born: Wilkinstown. Baptised: Oristown, 25 October 1891. Son of James and Ellen McCann, *née* Wilson, Demailstown, Wilkinstown. Father's occupation: Agricultural Labourer. Enlistment location: Navan. Killed in action, France & Flanders, 15 September 1916. Age: 25. Memorial: XXXIII.A.4, Serre Road Cemetery No. 2.

McCLOREY, Owen: Private, Royal Irish Regiment, 7th Battalion, 18172. Formerly Leinster Regiment, 5195. Born: Co. Down. Son of John and Anne McClorey, Dunshaughlin and later of Towns Park, Athboy. Father's occupation: Baker. Occupation: Groom. Residence: Athboy. Enlistment location: Mullingar. Killed in action, France & Flanders, 21 March 1918. Memorial: VI.B.5, Villers-Bretonneaux Military Cemetery.

McCONNON, James: Gunner, Royal Field Artillery, 76th Battery. 65553. Baptised: Slane, 3 October 1889. Son of Terence and Mary Anne McConnon, *née* Timmins, Slane. Father's occupation: Shoemaker. Occupation: Labourer, Copper Miner. Enlistment location: Drogheda. Died: Mesopotamia, 3 September 1916. Age: 26. Memorial: XXI.E.26, Baghdad

(North Gate) War Cemetery, Iraq. Drogheda War Memorial.

McCONNON, Matthew J.: Private, Irish Guards, 1st Battalion, 5162. Born: Drogheda, Co. Meath. Enlistment location: Drogheda. Served in France from 4 February 1915. Killed in action, France & Flanders, 16 March 1915. Memorial: I.D.14, Guards Cemetery, Windy Corner, Cuinchy. Drogheda War Memorial.

McCONNON, William: Private, Lancashire Fusiliers, 2nd/5th Battalion, 303020. Formerly Liverpool Regiment, 35720. Born: Slane, 17 November 1897. Son of Bernard and Margaret McConnon, *née* Caffrey, Coalpits, Slane. Father's occupation: Farmer. Enlistment location: Liverpool. Killed in action, France & Flanders, 31 July 1917. Memorial: Panel 33, Ypres (Menin Gate) Memorial. Drogheda War Memorial.

McCORMACK, Henry Michael: Private, Royal Dublin Fusiliers, 8th Battalion, 23221. Born: Co. Kildare. Husband of Margaret McCormack, *née* Woods, 2 Boyne Cottages, Trim. Occupation: Boot and Shoemaker. Residence: Trim. Died of wounds, France & Flanders, 21 July 1916. Age: 41. Memorial: Newtown Cemetery, Trim. From Newtown cemetery, Trim, '23221 Private Henry McCormack, Royal Irish Fusiliers, 21 July 1916 age 41.' From Trim Church of Ireland, Roll of Honour, 'McCormack, H. Private, Royal Dublin Fusiliers.'

McCORMICK, John Hugh Gardiner: Captain, Royal Warwickshire Regiment, 4th Battalion, attached 2nd Battalion. Born: Co. Dublin. Son of Samuel and Emily McCormick, Shandon, Monkstown, Co. Dublin. Father's occupation: Justice of the Peace, Annuities and Dividends. Occupation: Army Special Reserve and Farmer. Died: France & Flanders, 19 October 1914. Age: 28. Memorial: Panel 8, Ypres (Menin Gate) Memorial. In 1912 John McCormick of Monkstown, Dublin purchased Williamstown House, Kells and 127 acres. In August 1914 John enlisted and three weeks later was reported missing, and following interviewing a number of soldiers the family eventually accepted that he was dead. Six months later his brother, Jim, was also killed in the war. Their sister, Rose, made her home at Williamstown house and lived there until her death in 1972. From Brass Lectern: Kells church, formerly in Moynalty church, and moved to Kells church in 1992, 'Sine Timore. To the Glory of God and in loving memory of John Hugh Gardiner McCormick of Williamstown, Co. Meath. Captain, Royal Warwick Regt. He was mortally wounded in action. Oct. 19th. 1914, and died the same night at a Convent Hospital in German hands at Menin. Aged 28 years. Fear God and keep his Commandments.' Captain J.H.G. McCormick, Royal Warwickshire Regt (War Memorial, 1914-1918, Kells Church of Ireland).

McCORMACK, Thomas: Private, Irish Guards, 1st Battalion, 8125. Baptised: Kells, 10 October 1889. Son of John and Rose McCormack, *née* Cregan, Market Street, Kells. Father's occupation: Shopkeeper. Occupation: Shop Assistant. Residence: Kells. Enlistment location: Dublin. Killed in action, France & Flanders, 30 November 1917. Age: 27. Memorial: Panel 2 and 3, Cambrai Memorial, Louveral. From the *Meath Chronicle*, 27 November 1915:

Four Sons in the Army - Kells Lady Complimented.
Mrs McCormack, Market St Kells has received the following letter:-

Headquarters, Irish Command, Parkgate st. Dublin. 17th November 1915.
Madam – It has been brought to the notice of the General Officer commanding-in-chief the forces in Ireland that you have now four sons serving in the army, all of whom have given up good positions in civil life in order to serve their country. I am directed, therefore, by the Commander-in-Chief to congratulate you upon the loyalty and self-sacrifice of your sons, to wish you happiness in the future, and a safe return of each one of your family. It is the earnest hope of the Commander of the Forces that the fine example set by your sons will be followed by those in the district who have not yet realised their duty to their country. I am, Madam, your obedient Servant, Cecil Stafford, Aide-de-Camp.

From the *Meath Chronicle*, 22 December 1917:

Death of Kells Man in France
It is with feelings of regret we chronicle the death of Pte. Thomas McCormack of the Irish Guards, son of Mrs McCormack, Market Street, Kells, which occurred as a result of the recent activity on the Western Front. Deceased who had been engaged as a commercial traveller, joined up at an early stage of the war and having been trained at the Guards Depot in Caterham, saw many months of active service. He was gassed early in the spring of the present year and had only been in France a very short time after his recovery when he met his untimely end. He was educated at the Christian Brothers Schools, Kells and received his commercial training in a well-known Kells establishment. The sad news of his death has evoked widespread regret and sympathy with his mother and relatives in Kells district where he was deservedly popular. R.I.P.

McDERMOTT, Matthew: Private, Leinster Regiment, 7th Battalion, 2895. Born: Kells. Living: Broxburn, Hertfordshire. Enlistment location: Broxburn. Killed in action, France & Flanders, 3 September 1916. Memorial: Pier and Face 16C, Thiepval Memorial.

McDONALD, Alexander: Private, Royal Dublin Fusiliers, 9th Battalion, 25115. Born: Co. Dublin. Son of Donald and Elizabeth MacDonald, Laytown Station. Father's occupation: Railway Station Master. Enlistment location: Dublin. Killed in action, France & Flanders, 16 August 1917. Age: 18. Memorial: Panel 144 to 145, Tyne Cot Memorial. Drogheda War Memorial.

McDONNELL, James: Private, Leinster Regiment, 2nd Battalion, 7435. Baptised: Kells, 28 August 1887. Son of James and Maggie McDonnell, *née* Latimer, Cannon Street, Kells. Father's occupation: Car Owner. Married Rose Anne McCabe, at Kells, 15 November 1911. Residence: Church Lane, Kells. Enlistment location: Navan. Died of wounds, France & Flanders, 5 April 1915. Memorial: J.62, Bailleul Communal War Cemetery, (Nord). From the *Meath Chronicle*, 10 April 1915:

Kells Soldier Seriously Wounded
The chaplain (Rev. Fr. Bailey) at a casualty clearing station at the front has written a sympathetic letter to Mrs McDonald, Church Lane, Kells, informing her that her husband, Private James McDonald, of the 2nd Leinsters, has been very seriously wounded by a shell, losing part of his right leg and sustaining severe injuries to the shoulder and arm. The injured soldier, who as a reservist, went out to the war in August, still lies in the field hospital, being apparently too ill to be removed to the hospital at the base.

From the *Meath Chronicle*, 17 April 1915:

Kells Soldier Killed in Action
Much sympathy will be felt with his widow and mother on the death of Private James McDonnell, of the 2nd Leinsters, who has died from wounds received in action during Holy Week. The widow of the deceased, Mrs Rose A. McDonnell, Church Avenue, Kells has received the following letter – Easter Day:

'Dear Madam, - Your husband is in the Clearing Station, wounded. I am afraid they are rather bad wounds and he has had to lose part of his right leg, but I am glad to say he is going on well, and he is a cheerful patient. We hope he may shortly be sent down to a base hospital, so do not write until you hear again. He wished me to write and tell you this. Yours truly,

C.H. Bailey, chaplain
No. 2 Casualty Clearing Station.

McDONNELL, John: Lieutenant-Colonel, Leinster Regiment, 5th Battalion. Secondary Regiment: Royal Inniskilling Fusiliers. Attached to 1st Battalion. Drogheda War Memorial. Son of Dr Robert and Susan McDonnell, *née* McCausland, Kilsharvan and 89 Merrion Square, Dublin. Born: Dublin, 2 November 1878. Educated King's College Cambridge (BA). Succeeded his uncle, James, to the Kilsharvan estate in 1904. In 1911 living at Kilsharvan. Married 30 July 1914 to Eva Margaret Senta, daughter of Robert D'Arcy Jameson, Esq., Delvin Lodge, Balbriggan, Co. Dublin. Their son, Robert Edward McDonnell, was killed in the Second World War. Letters from Lieutenant Colonel John McDonnell to his wife while serving in France are now available in the National Library, Dublin. The letters mainly relate to family affairs and his health with some descriptions of conditions near Ypres. Some memorabilia belonging to John McDonnell is on display at Millmount, Drogheda. Killed in action, Ypres, France & Flanders, 29 September 1918. Age: 40. Memorial: II.D. 32, Ypres Reservoir Cemetery.

McDONNELL, Patrick: Private, Leinster Regiment, 2nd Battalion, 4239. Baptised: Navan, 20 February 1895. Son of John and Elizabeth McDonnell, *née* Foster, Watergate Street, later Infirmary Hill, later Old Cornmarket, Navan. Father's occupation: General Labourer. Enlistment location: Drogheda. Killed in action, France & Flanders, 23 August 1916. Age: 20. Memorial: III.A.26, Peronne Road Cemetery, Maricourt.

McDONNELL, Patrick: Private, Royal Dublin Fusiliers, 8th Battalion, 23642. Born: Donore. Occupation: Farm Labourer. Residence: Oldbridge. Enlistment location: Drogheda. Killed in action, France & Flanders, 9 September 1916. Memorial: Pier and Face 16C, Thiepval Memorial. Drogheda War Memorial.

McENROE, Herbert Joseph: Assistant Steward, Mercantile Marine, SS *Pinegrove*, Glasgow. Baptised: Kells, 10 February 1899. Son of John and Catherine McEnroe, *née* O'Reilly, Kells and later of Leinster Street, Dublin; Vernon Street, Dublin and Sloperton Lodge, Kingstown, Co. Dublin. Father's occupation: (1901) Shopman, Tea Merchant, (1911) Commercial Traveller. Killed by mine, 11 December 1915. Age: 16. Memorial: Tower Hill Memorial.

McENROE, James: Private, Leinster Regiment, 7th Battalion, 5518. Baptised: Ballinlough, 12 April 1891. Son of Matthew and Mary McEnroe, *née* Duffy, Ballinlough, Kells. Father's occupation: Farmer. Husband of Mary

McEnroe, *née* Nolan, Dominick Street, Mullingar. Occupation: Agricultural Labourer. Residence: Multyfarnham. Enlistment location: Mullingar. Killed in action, France & Flanders, 7 June 1917. Memorial: II, AA. 8, La Laiterie Military Cemetery.

McEVOY, Patrick: Lance-Corporal, Irish Guards, 2nd Battalion, 6397. Baptised St Mary's, Drogheda, 10 November 1889. Son of Thomas and Kate McEvoy, *née* Rath, Donacarney, Drogheda. Father's occupation: Agricultural Labourer. Brother, Thomas, also killed in the war. Occupation: Labourer. Enlistment location: Drogheda. Served in France from 17 August 1915. Killed in action, France & Flanders, 16 October 1915. Age: 26. Memorial: Panel 9 and 10, Loos Memorial. Drogheda War Memorial.

McEVOY, Richard: Private, Irish Guards, Reserve Battalion, B Company, 3rd Battalion, 9396. Baptised: Lobinstown, 6 July 1879. Son of Owen and Catherine McEvoy, *née* Lynch, Rathbranbeg. Father's occupation: Farmer. Husband of A. McEvoy. Enlistment location: Drogheda. Accidentally killed while bomb-throwing in England. Died at home, 8 January 1916. Age: 36. Memorial: L.41, Great Warley (Christ Church) Cemetery.

McEVOY, Thomas: Lance-Sergeant, Irish Guards, 1st Battalion, 3930. Baptised: St Mary's, Drogheda, 25 September 1891. Son of Thomas and Kate McEvoy, *née* Rath, Donacarney, Drogheda. Father's occupation: Agricultural Labourer. Brother, Patrick, also killed in the war. Occupation: Labourer. Married December 1915. Husband of Mary Ellen McEvoy, Woodside, Bettystown, Drogheda. Served in France from 13 August 1914. Died of wounds, France & Flanders, 3 December 1917. Age: 26. Award: Military Medal. Memorial: III.E.8, Tincourt New British Cemetery. Drogheda War Memorial.

McGRANE, Peter: Private, Royal Dublin Fusiliers, 6th Battalion, 22058. Formerly Leinster Regiment, 1869. Baptised: Stamullin, 18 May 1895. Son of Denis and Margaret McGrane, *née* Russell, Smithstown. Father's occupation: Shepherd. Brother, William, killed 1918. Occupation: Agricultural Labourer. Residence: Julianstown. Enlistment location: Drogheda. Served in Balkans from 7 August 1915. Killed in action, Balkans, 3 October 1916. Memorial: III.B.13, Struma Military Cemetery, Greece. Drogheda War Memorial. From *Drogheda Independent*, 28 November 1916:

Mrs McGrane, Julianstown, whose son, Peter, has been killed in action, has received the following letter from the lieutenant of the platoon in which this brave young soldier served: "Dear Madam – I am very sorry to have to inform you that your son, No 22028 Pte. P. McGrane, of A Coy, of the 6th Royal Dublin Fusiliers, has been killed in action on the 3rd of this month. He was acting as my orderly at the time, and showed the utmost coolness and bravery under fire, and in fact, was all that you and his country could have wished. It occurred during a strong Bulgar counter attack on a position which we had captured previously. Your son with several others, including myself, were hastening to reinforce the line, when he was killed. I sincerely hope it may alleviate your trouble in some small degree to learn that he died instantaneously and without pain, being shot through the heart. In all probability further particulars will be supplied to you later. Please accept my real sympathy for your loss. I remain his platoon officer, C. Byron, Lieut., attached 6th R.D.F., Salonica Forces.

McGRANE, William: Private, Royal Irish Fusiliers, 9th Battalion, 10752. Baptised: Stamullin, 26 July 1891. Son of Denis and Margaret McGrane, née Russell, Smithstown. Father's occupation: Shepherd. Brother, Peter, killed 1916. Residence: Julianstown. Enlistment location: Drogheda. Served in France from 19 December 1914. Killed in action, France & Flanders, 19 April 1918. Age: 27. Memorial: Panel 140 to 141, Tyne Cot Memorial. Drogheda War Memorial.

McGRATH, Richard: Private, Leinster Regiment, 1st Battalion, 9525. Born: Slane, 30 May 1893. Son of Thomas and Bridget McGrath, née Sheridan, Slane and later of Irishtown, Mountmellick, Co. Laois. Enlistment location: Maryborough. Killed in action, France & Flanders, 19 April 1915. Memorial: I.G.6, Ypres Town Cemetery Extension.

McGUINNESS, Michael: Private, Cameron Highlanders, 5th Battalion, S/22787. Born: Meath. Residence: Wanishaw, Lanarkshire. Enlistment location: Hamilton, Lanarkshire. Killed in action, France & Flanders, 20 September 1917. Memorial: XLIV.A.28, Tyne Cot Cemetery.

McGUIRE, Joseph: Private, Royal Irish Regiment, 7th Battalion, 11664. Formerly Royal Dublin Fusiliers, 25647. Baptised: Oldcastle, 4 November 1896. Son of Elizabeth McGuire, Church Street, Bailieborough, Co. Cavan. Enlistment location: Naas. Died of wounds, France & Flanders, 15 October 1918. Age: 21. Memorial: IV.B.9, La Kreule Military Cemetery, Hazlebrouk.

McGUIRE, William: Private, King's Own (Royal Lancaster Regiment), 6th Battalion, 20962. Son of Joseph McGuire, Trim. Husband of Sarah Eleanor McGuire, née Chadwick, 4, Havelock Road, Windermere, Cumbria. William McGuire married

Sarah Eleanor Chadwick 21 October 1908 in Tickley, Leicestershire. Their daughter, Eleanor Jean, was born 11 February 1910 in Adelaide, South Australia. Their second daughter, Mary Isabel Madigan Maguire, was born 22 March 1912. Residence: Wharton House, Cartwel, Grange-over-Sands, Lancashire. Age at enlistment: 38 years. Occupation: Painter, grainer and decorator. Died of acute gastritis due to field operation, 17 July 1916, Bombay, India. Age: 39. His wife later applied to have the cost of the journey from Australia to England in 1915 refunded by the military but this was refused as McGuire had not joined up within two months of returning from Australia. Memorial: Face B, Kirkee 1914-1918 Memorial.

McGUIRES, S.: Private, Leinster Regiment, 5th Battalion, 5017. Born: Athboy. Son of Mr J. McGuires, Ballyboy, Athboy. Died at home, 17 May 1916. Memorial: E.13.50, Naas (St Corban's) Catholic Cemetery.

McINERNEY: Gunner. From the *Meath Chronicle*, 30 June 1917, 'The death in action is announced of Gunner McInerney, RFA, a son of the late Bernard McInerney, stationmaster at Navan GNR and a native of Fordstown, Kells.' Possibly Charles W. McInerney, Bombardier Royal Field Artillery, C Battery, 298th Brigade, 711792. Born: Dublin. Killed in action, France, 9 May 1917. Memorial: VI.L.14, Vlamertinghe Military Cemetery.

McKENNA, Denis: Private, Royal Inniskilling Fusiliers, 1st Battalion, 27693. Born: Meath. Brother of Mrs Mary McKenna, 15 North Richmond Street, Dublin. Enlistment location: Glasgow. Killed in action, France & Flanders, 30 November 1917. Memorial: Panel 5 and 6, Cambrai Memorial, Louveral.

McKEON, James: Private, Irish Guards, 2nd Battalion, 8472. Born: Stamullin. Killed in action, France & Flanders, 13 September 1917. Memorial: VIII.E.8, Artillery Wood Cemetery.

McKEON, John: Private, Leinster Regiment, 7th Battalion, 5/5036. Baptised: Duleek, 22 February 1880. Son of Matthew and Anne McKeon, *née* Byrne, Downstown, Duleek. Father's occupation: Farm Labourer. Living: Duleek. Occupation: Shepherd. Enlistment location: Drogheda. Killed in action, France & Flanders, 17 April 1916. Age: 28. Memorial: II.K.30, Vermelles British Cemetery. Drogheda War Memorial.

McKEOWN, Henry: Sergeant, Australian Infantry, AIF, 4th Battalion, 1151. Formerly served in Leinster Regiment, 2nd Battalion for nine years. Baptised: St Mary's, Drogheda, 2 May 1874. Son of Henry and Margaret

McKeown, *née* Johnston. Occupation: Marine Fireman. Height: 5 foot 6 inches. Eyes: Blue. Hair: Brown. Enlisted 28 September 1914. Killed in action, Gallipoli, between 6 and 8 August 1915. Age: 39. Memorial III.B.32, Lone Pine Cemetery, Anzac.

McLARNEY, John: Private, Leinster Regiment, 7th Battalion, 4981. Baptised: Oldcastle, 30 January 1896. Son of James and Anne McElarney, *née* Corr, Moate, Ballinacree, Oldcastle. Residence: Oldcastle. Enlistment location: Navan. Killed in action, France & Flanders, 23 October 1916. Age: 20. Memorial: VII.C.2, La Laiterie Military Cemetery.

McLOUGHLIN, James: Lance-Corporal, Royal Irish Fusiliers, 1st Battalion, 20413. Born: Oristown. Son of John and Margaret McLoughlin, Ardbraccan and later Tankardstown, Donaghpatrick, Navan. Father's occupation: Farm Labourer. Residence: Navan. Enlistment location: Drogheda. Killed in action, France & Flanders, 24 June 1917. Age: 19. Memorial: Bay 9, Arras Memorial.

McLOUGHLIN, Thomas: Private, Royal Dublin Fusiliers, 2nd Battalion, 9165. Born: Dunboyne. Residence: Dunboyne. Enlistment location: Dublin. Killed in action, France & Flanders, 30 January 1915. Memorial: I.A.33, Porte-de-Paris Cemetery, Cambrai.

McMAHON, Joseph: Private, Leinster Regiment, 2nd Battalion, 9993. Born: Kells. Enlistment location: Drogheda. Served in France from 8 September 1914. Killed in action, France & Flanders, 20 October 1914. First battle of the 2nd Battalion, took place 18-20 October 1914 at Armentieres. Memorial: III.J.21, White House Cemetery, St Jean-les-Ypres. From the *Meath Chronicle*, 28 November 1914, 'Meathmen Killed and Wounded. Joseph McMahon, Kells of the Connaught Rangers, is reported to have been killed at the war. From the *Meath Chronicle*, 26 December 1914:

A Fighting Kells Family
James McMahon of Kells, who was a few weeks ago hit by a shell at one of the great river battles of France, returned home on Saturday night, looking little the worse of his wounds. He belongs to the Connaught Rangers, and was with that famous fighting regiment in India for a few years before the outbreak of the war. He has endured many hardships at the front, but is such a seasoned soldier that he took them as a matter of course. He saw many German youths of 16 to 18 years of age in the trenches and describes their condition as pitiable. McMahon's brother, Joseph, who joined the Leinsters before the war, and who volunteered for the front, was

shot dead at the Battle of Mons. A younger brother, Paddy, who is in the Leinsters, left Ireland with a company for the war last week. There are not many families in Meath who can point to such a record in connection with the war as the McMahons. Matty McMahon, uncle of the soldiers, was himself a soldier, and went through the South African War with the Connaughts. He was a very useful footballer in his time, and played with the Gladstone Home Rulers, and subsequently with the Kells Campaigners, among whom he was regarded as a very good forward.

McMANUS, James: Private, Leinster Regiment, 2nd Battalion, 5216. Baptised: Trim, 15 September 1898. Son of Patrick and Ellen McManus, *née* Cosgrave, Dalystown, Castlerickard. Father's occupation: Farmer and Agricultural Labourer. His brother, Patrick, also served with the Leinsters and was wounded by a bullet through the knee. Surviving the war, he died in 1978. Their cousin, William Smyth, Donore, Ballivor, was also killed in the war. Enlistment location: Mullingar. Died of wounds, France & Flanders, 4 June 1918. Age: 19. Memorial: I.F.24, Ebblinghem Military Cemetery. Award: Military Medal. McManus, James Cpl DCM Leinster Regiment, Trim Church of Ireland, Roll of Honour.

McPARTLAND, John: Private, Royal Dublin Fusiliers, 8th Battalion, 20013. Born: Kells. Brother, Matthew, killed 1915. Residence: Kells. Enlistment location: Dublin. Served in France from 20 December 1915. Killed in action, France & Flanders, 27 April 1916. Memorial: Panel 127 to 129, Loos Memorial. From the *Meath Chronicle*, 27 May 1916:

Killed in action
News has reached Kells that on April 27th John McPartland of the Dublin Fusiliers was killed while serving with his regiment in France. Some time previously his brother, Matthew, who belonged to the Irish Guards, also fell fighting in France. They were the sons of Mrs Pat Keenan, Newmarket Street, with whom sympathy will be felt in her heavy affliction.

McPARTLAND, Matthew: Private, Irish Guards, 2nd Battalion, 7985. Born: Lurgan, Co. Cavan. Brother, John, killed 1916. Enlistment location: Dublin. Served in France from 6 October 1915. Killed in action, France & Flanders, 18 October 1915. Memorial: I.H.8, Vermelles British Cemetery. From the *Meath Chronicle*, 27 May 1916:

Killed in action
News has reached Kells that on April 27th John McPartland of the Dublin Fusiliers was killed

while serving with his regiment in France. Some time previously his brother, Matthew, who belonged to the Irish Guards, also fell fighting in France. They were the sons of Mrs Pat Keenan, Newmarket Street, with whom sympathy will be felt in her heavy affliction.

McPHILLIPS, Joseph: Rifleman, Royal Irish Rifles, 7th Battalion, 3930. Born: Ballyjamesduff, Co. Cavan. Son of Hugh and Catherine McPhillips, Fennor Lower, Oldcastle. Father's occupation: General Labourer. Occupation: Labourer. Residence: Oldcastle. Enlistment location: Drogheda. Killed in action, France & Flanders, 9 September 1916. Age: 29. Memorial: Pier and Face 4D and 5B, Thiepval Memorial.

McWHIRTER, Robert P.: Private, Argyll and Sutherland Highlanders, 10th Battalion, S/9419. Born: Kells. Son of Mary McWhirter. Occupation: Farmer. Residence: Lossett, Moybologue. Residence: New Galloway, Kilcudbrights. Enlistment location: Dumfries, Dumfriesshire. Served in France from 14 October 1915. Killed in action, France & Flanders, 19 July 1916. Memorial: Pier and Face 15A and 16C, Thiepval Memorial.

MADDEN, Patrick Joseph: Private, Royal Dublin Fusiliers, 10th Battalion, 26425. Born: Branganstown. Son of Nicholas and Rose Madden, Branganstown, Kilmessan. Father's occupation: Farmer. Residence: Branganstown. Occupation: Farmer's son. Enlistment location: Greenock. Died of wounds, France & Flanders, 22 February 1917. Age: 23. Memorial: I.D.5, Mont Huon Military Cemetery, Le Treport.

MAGAN, Frederick: Private, 8th King's Royal Irish Hussars or No. 2 Cavalry Depot. 24306. Son of William and Mary Jane Magan, Kingsfort, Moynalty, later of Allenstown, Martry and later of Main Street, Celbridge, Co. Kildare. Father's occupation: (1901) Coachman, (1911) Stud Groom. Residence: Celbridge. Enlistment location: Dublin. Died at home from illness contracted on active service, 27 February 1915. Age: 21. Memorial: New Ground, 51, Donacomper Cemetery, Celbridge.

MAGUIRE, Andrew: Private, Leinster Regiment, 7th Battalion, 5172. Baptised: Trim, 9 July 1889. Son of James and Elizabeth Maguire, *née* Pepper, Church Street, Trim. Father's occupation: Dealer. Occupation: General Labourer. Residence: Navan. Enlistment location: Navan. Killed in action, France & Flanders, 16 October 1917. Age: 28. Memorial: Arras Memorial. 'Maguire, A. Private, Leinster Regiment' (Trim Church of Ireland, Roll of Honour). From the *Meath Chronicle*, 5 June 1915, 'A Trim soldier named Maguire has had a narrow escape from death in the trenches, a bullet taking his belt pouch away.'

MAGUIRE, George Joseph: Private, Leinster Regiment, 2nd Battalion, 5687. Reservist. Baptised: Kells, 13 January 1881. Son of Bernard and Mary Maguire, *née* Gerety, New Rath, Loyd, Kells. Father's occupation: Farm Labourer. His brothers, Edward and Bernard, also enlisted. Edward was wounded at Salonica in 1916 and Bernard was wounded in France in 1916. Enlistment location: Navan. Served in the Boer War, 1899-1902. Died of wounds, France & Flanders, 30 October 1915. Age: 33. Memorial: IV.C.6, Lijssenthoek Military Cemetery. From the *Meath Chronicle*, 16 October 1915, 'George and Edward Maguire of Loyd, Kells, of the Leinster Regiment, who were home on leave, returned to the war on Monday, the former to France and the latter to the Dardanelles.' From the *Meath Chronicle*, 6 November 1915:

Kells Soldier Killed in France
During the week official intimation came of the death from wounds of Private George Maguire of the Leinster regiment, who was home recently for a few days. He went back last Monday fortnight and soon afterwards was seriously wounded in the chest on going into action. He lingered for a few days, during which the Regimental Chaplain, Abbe L'Berghen, was constantly in attendance and was at his bedside in his dying moments. The deceased, who has two brothers in the army – one of whom, Edward, has been wounded in the Dardanelles – was son of Mr. Bernard and Mrs Maguire, Loyd, and with them and the members of the family great sorrow sincere sympathy is felt.

Abbe L'Berghen in a letter dated October 31st to poor Maguire's father wrote:- "I gave him Absolution and Extreme Unction on Thursday. He was a little better on Friday but yesterday he had more and more trouble to breathe. I gave him a Crucifix in order to help him and he kissed it. I spoke to him till yesterday at 8 o'clock in the evening but he was very sleepy. Soon after, without any suffering, he passed away and received from God the reward which is reserved to those who do their duty even unto death. I will bury him this afternoon in the little cemetery which is near our hospital, and a cross with his name will be put on his grave. I beg you to accept my deep sympathy in your great misfortune. You will find in his belongings which are sent to you the Crucifix which was kissed before his death.

MAGUIRE, Patrick: Private, Leinster Regiment, 6th Battalion, 468.

Born: Kells. Carnaross. Enlistment location: Drogheda. Served in Balkans from 5 August 1915. Killed in action, Gallipoli, 9 August 1915. Memorial: Sp. Mem. C. 9, Embarkation Pier Cemetery.

MAHON, Hugh: Private, The Border Regiment, 1st Battalion, 28717. Formerly Royal Army Service Corps, T/4/086256. Born: Oldcastle. Mother: Mary Mahon, Oldcastle. Husband of Nora Mahon, 321, East 65th Street, New York City, USA. Residence: Oldcastle. Enlistment location: Dundalk. Served in the Balkans. Killed in action, France & Flanders, 31 July 1917. Age: 37. Memorial: Panel 35, Ypres (Menin Gate) Memorial.

MAHON, Matthew J.: Private, Irish Guards, 2nd Battalion, 12151. Baptised: Ballivor, 14 November 1888. Son of John and Mary Mahon, née Duffy, Coolronan, Ballivor. Father's occupation: Farmer. Occupation: Farmer's son. Husband of Kate Mahon, 11 Lower Abbey Street, Dublin. Enlistment location: Dublin. Killed in action, France & Flanders, 23 March 1918. Age: 30. Memorial: Bay 1, Arras Memorial.

MALONE, Patrick: Rifleman, Royal Irish Rifles, 2nd Battalion, 7254. Born: Dunboyne. Son of Thomas and Mary Malone, 7 Sullivan Street, Infirmary Road, Dublin. Enlistment location: Dublin. Served in France from 15 August 1914. Killed in action, France & Flanders, 26 October 1914. Age: 30. Memorial: Panel 42 and 43, Le Touret Memorial.

MALONE, William: Sergeant, Royal Dublin Fusiliers, 2nd Battalion, 7522. Born: Dublin. Husband of Rose Malone, Brannixtown, Trim. Enlistment location: Dublin. Served in France from 20 September 1914. Killed in action, France & Flanders, 24 May 1915. Age: 34. Memorial: Panel 44 and 46 Ypres (Menin Gate) Memorial.

MANNING, Frank: Leinster. Crossakeel, killed. (Horneck)

MARKEY, John: Private, Australian Trench Mortar Battery, 3rd Brigade, 2214. Baptised Kilbeg 10 August 1882. Son of Thomas and Kate Markey, née Kelry, Togherstown and later of Ipswich Road, Brisbane, Queensland. Brother, Thomas, also killed in the war. Height: 5 foot 8 inches. Eyes: Grey. Hair: Auburn. Occupation: Freezer. Enlisted: 28 July 1915. Enlistment location: Brisbane. Served in France from 3 April 1916. Died of sickness, Frances & Flanders, 6 June 1916. Memorial: II.T.7, Estaires Communal Cemetery and Extension.

MARKEY, Thomas: Private, Australian Infantry, AIF, 25th Battalion, 1713. Baptised: Kilbeg 20 January 1882. Son of Thomas and Kate Markey, *née* Kelry, Togherstown and later of Ipswich Road, Brisbane, Queensland. Brother, John, also killed in the war. Height: 5 foot 8 inches. Eyes: Grey. Hair: Brown. Occupation: Carpenter. Enlisted 1 June 1915. Enlistment location: Brisbane. Served in Gallipoli from 12 October 1915. Served in France from 14 March 1916. Wounded in action 29 July 1916. Killed in action, France & Flanders, 14 November 1916. Memorial: III.A.13, Wallencourt British Cemetery.

MARLOW, Charles Dwyer: Second Lieutenant, Royal Dublin Fusiliers, formerly Private, 3644, 28th London Regiment and Artists' Rifles, 8th Battalion. Born 14 October 1894. Son of Arthur and Amelia Frances Marlow, *née* Griffith, Oldcastle and later Clonlyne, Penrhyn Bay, Llandudno, Carnarvonshire. Father's occupation: National School Teacher. Mother's occupation: National School Teacher. Educated at Blue Coat School, King's Hospital, 1909-13. Served in France from 11 August 1915. Commissioned 18 September 1916. Killed in action, France & Flanders, 17 August 1917. Memorial: Panel 144 to 145, Tyne Cot Memorial. Tablet in St Bride Church of Ireland church, Oldcastle, 'Memorial to Charles Dwyer Marlow, Oldcastle 2nd Lieutenant 8th Royal Dublin Fusiliers, previously of the Artists Rifles. Killed in action at Frezenberg 17th August 1917 aged 22 years.'

MARSHALL-BARNES, Alfred Hubert: Private, 62nd Canadian Field Ambulance, Royal Army Medical Corps. 33207. Born: Sandgate. Son of the late Lieutenant-Colonel Lionel Marshall, Lancashire Fusiliers. Husband of Hester F. Marshall-Barnes, Westland, Moynalty. Killed in action, Somme, 2 September 1916. Age: 34. Memorial: O.31, Carnoy Military Cemetery.

MASTERSON, Michael: Private, Leinster Regiment, 2nd Battalion, 2201. Baptised Navan, 11 August 1884. Son of Christopher and Elizabeth Masterson, *née* McGovern, Barrack Lane, Navan. Father's occupation: Labourer. Husband of Mary Ann Masterson, 36 St Finian's Terrace, Navan. Two children: Frederick and Lizzie. Occupation: Labourer. Worked for Navan Urban District Council. Enlistment location: Mosney. Served in France from 26 October 1914. Died of wounds, France & Flanders, 12 May 1915. Memorial: I.C.19, Erquingham-Lys Churchyard Extension Cemetery. From the *Meath Chronicle*, 22 May 1915:

Navan Soldier killed in the War
Mrs Masterson, Navan, received word on Monday of the death of her husband, Michael Masterson, 2nd Leinsters, on the 12th inst. A brother of the deceased is in the same regiment and writing to Mrs Masterson about her husband's death, says he died in Paris after

being wounded and had the priest before he died and was conscious to the last. Deceased was a well-known Navan man and his death has occasioned much sorrow all over the town.

MASTERSON, Michael: Private, Irish Guards, 1st Battalion, 5597. Born: Kells. Son of Mrs Mary Masterson, Oakley Park, Kells. Enlistment location: Navan. Served in France from 25 May 1915. Killed in action, France & Flanders, 23 October 1915. Age: 19. Memorial: I.H.2, Vermelles British Cemetery.

MASTERSON, Patrick: Private, Leinster Regiment, 7th Battalion, 3704. Born: Navan. Son of Christopher Masterson. Husband of Mary Masterson *née* Brady, Trimgate Street, Navan. Enlistment location: Navan. Killed in action, France & Flanders, 17 August 1917. Age: 37. Memorial: Panel 143, Tyne Cot Memorial.

MASTERSON, Patrick: Private, Royal Irish Fusiliers, 1st Garrison Battalion, G/694. Formerly Leinster Regiment, 3941. Born: Navan. Husband of Mary Masterson, Circular Road, Navan, Co. Meath. Served in the South African War. Died at sea, on HS *Delia* 7 August 1916. Award: Long service and good conduct medal. Memorial: Hollybrook Memorial, Southampton.

MATHIESON, Kenneth Ronald: Lieutenant, Irish Guards, 1st Battalion. Son of Kenneth and Margaret Mathieson, Tara Hall and 50 Prince's Gate, South Kensington, London. Rejoined regiment on the outbreak of war. Served in France from 11 September 1914. Killed in action, near Ypres, 1 November 1914. Age: 28. Memorial: Panel 11, Ypres (Menin Gate) Memorial. From the *Meath Chronicle*, 21 November 1914:

Sportsmen Killed in the War
That the Meath Hunt is suffering its own share as a result of the war is further exemplified by the sad news that several of its prominent followers have been killed while in action. Among the list of the dead published recently are Capt. F. Browning, R.F.A, Dundalk, Capt Ford, Hon. W.R. Wyndham, 17th Lancers; Lieutenant Matheson, K.R.F. Tara Hall; F.H.B. Blaithwayt, 2nd Life Guards; Lieut. Ballayxe, 11th Hussars; Lionel H. Partry, 5th Dragoon Guards; and Lieut. Legge Burke, Coldstream Guards, Hayes, Beauparc, nephew and successor to the late Hon. Harry Burke. The deceased officers, some used to stay at the Club, Navan were ardent and popular followers of the Meaths, and are deeply regretted by all who knew them.

MATTHEWS, John: *see* **Cahill, John.**

MATTOCK, Robert Clement: Corporal, Canadian Infantry, Central Ontario Regiment, 20th Battalion, 404889. Native of Taunton. Son of Robert Southwood and Elizabeth Mattock, Legar House, Hill of Down. Brother, Thomas, also killed in the war. Father's occupation: Estate Steward. Killed in action, France & Flanders, 15 September 1916. Age: 28. Memorial: III.Q.24, Pozieres British Cemetery.

MATTOCK, Thomas Southwood: Corporal, Royal Inniskilling Fusiliers, 8th Battalion, 19016. Born Somerset. Son of Robert Southwood and Elizabeth Mattock, Legar House, Hill of Down. Brother, Robert, also killed in the war. Father's occupation: Estate Steward. Occupation: Gamekeeper. Residence: Clonard. Enlistment location: Drogheda. Killed in action, France & Flanders, 9 September 1916. Age: 24. Memorial: Pier and Face 4D and 5B, Thiepval Memorial.

MEEHAN, Patrick: Private, Royal Irish Fusiliers, 1st Battalion, 18688. Baptised Castletown-Kilpatrick 26 January 1883. Son of Michael and Marie Meehan, *née* Kevitt, Drakestown Wilkinstown, Navan. Father's occupation: Groom/Domestic Servant. Occupation: Agricultural Labourer. Enlistment location: Armagh. Killed in action, France & Flanders, 11 April 1917. Age: 34. Memorial: VII.C.33, Terlincthun British Cemetery, Wimille.

MEEHAN, Peter: Private, Irish Guards, 1st Battalion, 2841. Born: Kilbride, Dunboyne. Residence: Belgree. Member of the Irish National Volunteers. Enlistment location: Dublin. Served in France from 21 September 1914. Died of wounds, France & Flanders, 17 November 1914.

MEGAN, Lawrence: Private, Royal Dublin Fusiliers, 10th Battalion, 26835. Born: Enniskerry, Co. Wicklow. Son of Thomas Megan. Husband of Mrs Kate Megan, Wilkinstown, Navan. Residence: Navan. Enlistment location: Dublin. Killed in action, France & Flanders, 13 November 1916. Age: 35. Memorial: VII.B.5, Ancre British Cemetery, Beaumont-Hamel.

METGE, Rudolph Cole: Captain, Leinster Regiment, 5th Battalion. Born: Dublin. Baptised: Bective, 12 April 1881. Son of Robert Henry Metge. Father's occupation: Landowner and Member of Parliament for Meath, 1880-1882. Residence: Kilcarn. Occupation: (1901) Officer in the Leinsters, (1911) Land Agent. Married to Clementine Graham-Tole of Nenagh in 1916. Died: 4 October 1919. Memorial: St Mary's Church of Ireland Churchyard, Bective. Roll of Honour, St Mary's church, Navan.

MILLAR, John: Private, Cameron Highlanders, 6th Battalion, S/23837. Son of Thomas W. and Elizabeth Millar, Market Place, Langholm, Dumfriesshire. In 1901 Thomas, Elizabeth, John and family were living at Abbeylands, Navan. All were born in Scotland. Brother, William, also killed in the war. Father's occupation: Tweed Designer Wool. Occupation: Pattern Weaver Wool. Died: 28 March 1918. Age: 26. Memorial: Bay 9, Arras Memorial. Roll of Honour, St Mary's church, Navan.

MILLAR, William: Sergeant, Black Watch, Royal Highlanders, 10th Battalion, S/3863. Husband of Helen Millar, 11 Merry Street, Motherwell, Lanarkshire. Son of Thomas and Elizabeth Millar. In 1901 Thomas, Elizabeth, William and family were living at Abbeylands, Navan. All were born in Scotland. Brother, John, also killed in the war. Father's occupation: Tweed Designer Wool. Occupation: Pattern Weaver Wool. Died: 8 May 1917. Age: 24. Memorial: I.D.4, Doiran Military Cemetery. Roll of Honour, St Mary's church, Navan.

MILLS, Robert Sydney: Lieutenant, Canadian Army Service Corps, Training Depot. Born Kingstown, Co. Dublin, 17 April 1874. Son of James and Elizabeth Mills, Co. Meath. Occupation: Publishing Business. Husband of Nora Mills, 59 Yorkville Avenue, Toronto, Ontario. Enlisted: 24 March 1915. Enlistment location: Quebec. Height: 5 foot 8½ inches. Complexion: Fair. Eyes: Blue. Hair: Fair. Served in the Ashanti Rebellion of 1900. Died: 25 March 1916. Age: 42. Memorial: M.16, Shorncliffe Military Cemetery.

MINCH, John: Gunner, Royal Garrison Artillery, 1st/1st Lancashire Heavy Battery. 309029. Born: Oristown. Son of James and Rose Minch, Oristown and later 18A, Demense Street, Seacombe, Wallasey, Cheshire. Enlistment location: Liverpool. Died: France & Flanders, 22 June 1918. Memorial: V.C.10, Pernes British Cemetery.

MITCHELL, Christopher: Private, Royal Dublin Fusiliers, 9th Battalion, 24693. Baptised Curraha, 19 June 1898. Son of John and Rose Mitchell, *née* Clarke, Coolfore. Father's occupation: Agricultural Labourer. Residence: Curragha. Enlistment location: Drogheda. Killed in action, France & Flanders, 6 September 1916. Memorial: Pier and Face 16C, Thiepval Memorial.

MITCHELL, John: Private, Royal Dublin Fusiliers, 8th Battalion, 24985. Born: Curraha. Enlistment location: Drogheda. Killed in action, France & Flanders, 6 September 1916. Memorial: XXIV.C.4, Delville Wood Cemetery, Longueval.

MOLLOY, Thomas: Gunner, Royal Garrison Artillery, B27th Trench Mortar Battery, 572. Born: Kells. Son of Cornelius and Ellen Molloy, 53 Frederick Avenue, East Hamilton, Ontario, Canada and 3 Seafield, Bathgate. Residence: Bathgate, Linlithgow. Enlisted: 20 August 1914. Enlistment location: West Hartlepool. Age at enlistment: 33 years. Height 6 foot ½ inch. Eyes: Brown. Hair: Black. Occupation: Navy. Had previously served with the Irish Guards. Served in France from 16 January 1916. Died of wounds, No. 10 Casualty Clearing Station, France, 5 March 1916. Age: 36. His personal effects including an identity disc, a gospel, a rosary, two religious emblems and a bag were returned to his father. Memorial: V.B.5, Lijssenthoek Military Cemetery.

MONAGHAN, Lawrence: Rough Rider, Royal Army Service Corps, 2nd Remount Depot, Woolwich, RTS/3228. Son of John Monaghan. Occupation: Groom. Enlisted: 8 October 1914. Enlistment location: Dublin. Age at enlistment: 30 years. Height: 5 foot 3½ inches. Eyes: Grey. Hair: Brown. In July 1918, a horse fell on him while schooling it and he was then hospitalised at Exeter War Hospital until his death on 23 February 1919. Age: 39. Memorial: Old Kilcarn Graveyard, Navan, close to north-west corner of the ruin.

MONAGHAN, Thomas: Private, Leinster Regiment, 2nd Battalion, 5769. Baptised: Navan, 8 April 1889. Son of John and Julia Monaghan, *née* Donoghue, Railway Street, Navan. Father's occupation: Labourer. Husband of Katie Monaghan, North Aston, Oxon. Enlistment location: Dublin. Died of wounds, France & Flanders, 2 October 1918. Age: 27. Memorial: V.C.32, Terlincthun British Cemetery, Wimille. From the *Meath Chronicle*, 12 October 1918, 'Prayers were offered at all Masses in Navan on Sunday for the repose of the soul of Thomas Monaghan, who was killed in the recent fighting. He is second eldest son of Mr. John Monaghan, Railway Street, Navan.'

MOONEY, James Private, North Staffordshire Regiment, 8th Battalion, 43029. Formerly Royal Dublin Fusiliers, 17607. Baptised: Dunboyne, 4 September 1888. Son of James and Bridget Mooney, *née* Connan. Occupation: Assistant Shepherd. Residence: Loughsallagh, Clonee. Enlistment location: Dublin. Killed in action, France & Flanders, 20 September 1917. Memorial: Panel 124 to 125 and 162 to 162A, Tyne Cot Memorial.

MOONEY, Michael: Private, Leinster Regiment, 2nd Battalion, 9785. Baptised: Trim, 19 September 1895. Son of James and Ellen Mooney, *née* Faulkner, Trim and later of 7

Parsons Street, Maynooth, Co. Kildare. Enlistment location: Drogheda, 1912. Served in France from 19 December 1914. Killed in action, France & Flanders, 15 March 1916. Age: 20. Memorial: Panel 44, Ypres (Menin Gate) Memorial.

MOORE, John: Private, Royal Dublin Fusiliers, 8th Battalion, 22473. Baptised: Castletown-Kilpatrick, 1 January 1891. Son of Thomas and Bridget Moore, *née* Reid, Knightstown, Wilkinstown. Mother's occupation: Railway Gate Keeper. Occupation: Farm Labourer. Enlistment location: Navan. Killed in action, France & Flanders, 8 September 1916. Age: 26. Memorial: Pier and Face 16C, Thiepval.

MOORE, Patrick: Private, Wiltshire Regiment, 5th Battalion, 23286. Born: Navan. Residence: Navan. Enlistment location: Aldershot. Killed in action, Mesopotamia, 25 January 1917. Memorial: Panel 30 and 64, Basra Memorial.

MORAN, W.: Leinster Regiment. Died: 1916. From the *Meath Chronicle*, 22 July, 'The names of J. Farrell (Kells), P. Irwin (do.), and W. Moran (Navan), of the Leinster Regiment appeared in Monday's list of casualties.'

MOSS, David: Private, Irish Guards, 2nd Battalion, 6671. Born: Loughcrew. Son of Adam and Mary Moss, Ballynamona, Loughcrew, Oldcastle and later 55, Vi Halton, Bryansburn, Bangor, Co. Down. Father's occupation: House Carpenter. Occupation: Labourer, Domestic Servant. Enlistment location: Drogheda. Served in France from 29 September 1915. Killed in action, France & Flanders, 23 March 1918. Age: 30. Memorial: Bay 1, Arras Memorial. Pte. David Moss – Irish Guards (First World War Memorial, St Kieran's church, Loughcrew).

MULALLEY, John: Private, Connaught Rangers, 2nd Battalion, B Company, 10444. Born: Enfield. Son of James and Mary Mulalley, Newcastle, Enfield. Residence: Enfield. Enlistment location: Naas, Co. Kildare. Served in France from 14 August 1914. Killed in action, France & Flanders, 7 November 1914. Age: 20. Memorial: Panel 42, Ypres (Menin Gate) Memorial.

MULDOON, Philip: Private, Leinster Regiment, 6th Battalion, 79. Baptised: Navan, 26 February 1876. Son of Patrick and Elizabeth Muldoon, *née* Smyth, Kilcarn. Enlistment location: Birr. Served in Balkans from 9 July 1915. Killed in action. Gallipoli, 11 August 1915. Age: 38. Memorial: Panel 184 and 185, Helles Memorial.

MULLEN, James Joseph: Corporal, 14th King's Hussars, 12362. Baptised: Kilcloon, 10 May 1888. Son of James and Annie Mullen, *née* McCormack,

Rodanstown, Kilcock. Twin of Mary Anne. Father's occupation: General Labourer. Brother, Patrick, also killed in the war. Residence: Kilcock. Enlistment location: Scarborough. Served in France from 22 June 1915. Died: Hamadan, Persia, 10 October 1918. Memorial: IV.C. 8, Teheran War Cemetery.

MULLEN, Patrick Joseph: Lance-Corporal, Royal Dublin Fusiliers, 8th Battalion, 16261. Baptised: Kilcloon, 17 March 1897. Son of James and Annie Mullen, née McCormack, Rodinstown, Kilcock. Father's occupation: General Labourer. Brother, James, also killed in the war. Residence: Kilcock, Co. Meath. Enlistment location: Naas, Co. Kildare. Served in France from 20 December 1915. Killed in action, France & Flanders, 27 April 1916. Age: 19. Memorial: Panel 127 to 129, Loos Memorial.

MULVANEY, James: Private, Royal Irish Fusiliers, 8th Battalion, A Company, 21996. Formerly 3673, Royal Irish Regiment. Born Kingstown (Dun Laoghaire), Co. Dublin. Son of Owen and Catherine Mulvaney, Kells. Killed in action, France & Flanders, 10 July 1916. Age: 24. Memorial: III.O.3, St Patrick's Cemetery, Loos.

MULVANEY, Joseph: Private, Canadian Infantry, British Columbia Regiment, 29th Battalion, 464219. Born: Mullingar, 14 July 1889. Son of Richard and Frances Mulvaney, née Fowler, Navan. Husband of Alice Mulvaney, née Hulme, Bolton Lancashire and Vancouver, British Columbia. Height 5 foot 5 inches. Eyes: Blue. Hair: Black. Enlisted 1 September 1915. Died: 21 August 1917. Age: 28. Memorial: Vimy Memorial.

MULVANEY, Thomas: Private, King's Own Yorkshire Light Infantry, 2nd/4th Battalion, 63419. Formerly Northumberland Fusiliers, 20/438. Born: Kells. Enlistment location: Newcastle-on-Tyne. Killed in action, France & Flanders, 4 November 1918. Memorial: I.B.13, Ruesnes Communal Cemetery.

MUNROE, Patrick: Private, King's Liverpool Regiment, 8th Battalion, 305149. Baptised Moynalty, 8 March 1896. Son of Patrick and Anne Munroe, née Farrelly, Baltrasna, Moynalty, later of Walterstown, Navan and later of 3 Tyrone Place, Golden Bridge, Inchicore, Dublin. Father's occupation: Farm Servant. Residence: Liverpool. Enlistment location: Liverpool. Served in France from 3 May 1915. Killed in action, France & Flanders, 28 September 1916. Age: 19. Memorial: Pier and Face 1D. 8B and 8C, Thiepval Memorial.

MUNRO, George: Private, Highland Light Infantry, 2nd/6th Battalion,

242006. Husband of Mary Hyslop Munro, 70 Crosbie Road, Troon, Ayrshire. Died at home, 17 June 1917. Memorial: Oldcastle Cemetery.

MURDOCK, Charles Walter: Private, Lothian and Border Horse, 1260. Born: Drogheda, Co. Louth. Son of Charles and Frances Jane Murdock, Irishtown, Rathfeigh. Father's occupation: Farmer. Residence: Edinburgh. Enlistment location: Edinburgh. Died: 8 October 1914. Age: 26. Memorial: K.839, Comely Bank Cemetery, Edinburgh. Drogheda War Memorial. From the *Drogheda Independent*, 10 October 1914, 'Murdock – October 8, 1914 at the Military Hospital … glaith of double pneumonia, Walter Charles, aged 25, only surviving son of Charles Murdock, Irishtown, Rathfeigh, Co. Meath.'

MURPHY, Christopher: Stoker, 1st Class, Royal Navy, HMS *Chelmer*. K/26523. Baptised: Enfield/Rathmolyon, 7 January 1887. Son of Thomas and Margaret Murphy, *née* Grehan, Newcastle, Enfield. Father's occupation: Shepherd. Died of pneumonia following influenza, Naval Hospital, Malta, 22 November 1918. Memorial: R.C.160, Capuccini Naval Cemetery, Malta.

MURPHY, Denis: Private, Leinster Regiment, 7th Battalion, 5326. Born: Athboy. Residence: Athboy. Enlistment location: Limerick. Killed in action, France & Flanders, 4 September 1916. Memorial: Pier and Face 16C, Thiepval Memorial.

MURPHY, George: Private, Leinster Regiment, 2nd Battalion, 5780. Baptised: Summerhill, 26 April 1889. Son of James O'Connell and Judith Murphy, *née* Cullen, Breemount, Trim. Married Ellen Maguire, 23 November 1910, St Patrick's church, Trim. Children: Mary, Ellen, Margaret and James: Occupation: Farmer. Residence: 37 Loman Street, Trim. Enlistment location: Drogheda. Killed in action, France & Flanders, 9 August 1918. Memorial: II.G.10, Borre British Cemetery. 'Pte George Murphy, Private, Leinster Regiment' (Trim Church of Ireland, Roll of Honour).

George Murphy. (Courtesy of May Ryan)

MURPHY, John: Private, Royal Dublin Fusiliers, 8th Battalion, 16602. Baptised: Kells, 27 August 1882. Son of Thomas and Margaret Murphy, *née* Tully, Kells and later of 83, Windmill Lane, Drogheda. Enlistment location: Coatsbridge. Killed in action, France & Flanders, 27 April 1916. Age: 33. Memorial: Panel 127 to 129, Loos Memorial.

MURPHY, Joseph: Rifleman, Royal Irish Rifles, 1st Battalion, 1321. Baptised: Navan, 30 May 1892. Son of Peter and Bridget Murphy, *née* Smith, Millbrook, Navan. Father's occupation: Labourer. Brother of John Murphy, Cannon Row, Navan. Occupation: Labourer. Enlistment location: Drogheda. Joined late in 1914. Served in France from 25 March 1915. Killed in action, France & Flanders, 9 May 1915. Memorial: Panel 9, Ploegsteert Memorial.

MURPHY, Michael: Private, Irish Guards, 1st Battalion, 8466. Baptised: Slane, 13 November 1884. Son of Andrew and Anne Murphy, *née* Hughes, Slane. Father's occupation: Tailor. Enlistment location: Drogheda. Killed in action, France & Flanders, 25 September 1916. Memorial: Pier and Face 7D, Thiepval Memorial.

MURPHY, Peter: Private, Leinster Regiment, 2nd Battalion, 5631. Born: Navan. Enlistment location: Navan. Killed in action, France & Flanders,

27 March 1918. Memorial: Panel 78, Pozieres Memorial.

MURRAY, John: Private, Leinster Regiment, 7th Battalion, 5340. Baptised: Kildalkey, 17 February 1889. Son of Christopher and Mary Murray, *née* Farrelly, Clonmore, Kildalkey. Father's occupation: Agricultural Labourer. Residence: Batterstown. Enlistment location: Drogheda. Killed in action, in battle for Guillemont, Somme, France, 3 September 1916. Memorial: Pier and Face 16C, Thiepval Memorial. From the *Meath Chronicle*, 'Mrs Anna M. Murray, Tribley, Kilmessan, has received the sad intelligence of the death of her husband, Mr. John Murray, in action. Deceased who was only 28 years of age belonged to the Leinster regiment and was killed in the big push of September 3rd.'

MURRAY, Patrick: Private, Irish Guards, 1st Battalion, 7887. Born: Oristown. Brother of Miss Mary Murray, Gibbstown, Navan. Enlistment location: Navan. Killed in action, France & Flanders, 27 August 1918. Memorial: Panel 3, Vis-en-Artois Memorial.

MURRAY, William Frederick: Private, Machine Gun Corps (Infantry), 1st Battalion, 36 Company, 46384. Formerly Middlesex Regiment, 3740. Born: Kells. Son of William Murray, Tipperary. Husband of Emily Maud Murray, 5 Belgrave Terrace, Stanhope Road, Finchley, London. Residence: Cricklewood. Enlistment location: Willesden Green. Killed accidentally, France & Flanders, 27 November 1916. Age: 34. Memorial: F.31, Agny Military Cemetery.

MURTAGH, James: Private, Royal Irish Regiment, 7th Battalion, 26565. Formerly Royal Dublin Fusiliers, 30296. Born: Meath. Residence: Chapel Brampton, Northamptonshhire. Enlistment location: Northampton. Killed in action, France & Flanders, 23 October 1918. Memorial: XXXII.A 6, Lijssenthoek Military Cemetery.

MURTAGH, William: Private, Irish Guards, 1st Battalion, No 4 Company, 3291. Baptised: Stamullin, 2 June 1889. Son of John and Josephine Murtagh, *née* Matthews, Gormanstown and later of New Cottages, Duleek Street, Drogheda, Co. Louth. Enlistment location: Drogheda. Served in France from 27 August 1914. Killed in action, France & Flanders, 17 February 1915. Age: 24. Memorial: II.D.4, Cuinchy Communal Cemetery.

N

NAPER, Francis C.: Captain, King's Own, Royal Lancaster Regiment. Son of Mrs Jane Naper, Norfolk House, Thames Embankment, London. Died: 3 May 1917. Age: 43. Memorial: B.10, Fampoux British Cemetery. 'Capt. Frank C. Naper 2nd K.O.R.L.' (First World War Memorial, St Kieran's church, Loughcrew).

NAPER, George Wyatt Edgell: Lieutenant-Commander, Royal Navy, HMS/M *E24*. Son of Lieutenant-Colonel W.D. Naper, Bayswater, London. Died: 27 March 1916. Memorial: 11, Portsmouth Naval Memorial. 'Lt-Com. George W.E. Naper R.N.' (First World War Memorial, St Kieran's church, Loughcrew).

NEVINS, Eugene: Private, Royal Inniskilling Fusiliers, 7th Battalion, 29909. Baptised: Navan, 20 October 1884. Son of Nicholas and Mary Nevins, *née* Duffy, Flowerhill, Navan. Father's occupation: Mill Manager. Residence: Shettleston. Enlistment location: Glasgow. Killed in action, France & Flanders, 16 August 1917. Memorial: Panel 70 to 72, Tyne Cot Memorial.

NOLAN: From the *Meath Chronicle*, 7 October 1916: 'Two soldiers from Trim district, named Duff and Nolan, are reported killed in action. This brings the total from Trim and its vicinity who have paid the supreme penalty up to fifteen.'

NORRIS, Reginald Walter: Second Lieutenant, Royal Air Force, No. 22 Training Depot Station RAF, Gormanstown. Killed on a training flight at Gormanstown, 20 October 1918. Memorial: St Mary's Churchyard, Julianstown.

NUGENT, Thomas: Lance-Corporal. Royal Irish Rifles, 2nd Battalion, 8873. Born: Westmeath. Son of Henry and Bridget Nugent, The Green, Trim. Father's occupation: Agricultural Labourer, Shepherd. Enlistment location: Athboy. Killed in action, France & Flanders, 15 July 1916. Age: 20. Memorial: II.G.3, Ovillers Military Cemetery.

NULTY, Edmund Christopher: Private, Royal Dublin Fusiliers, 10th Battalion, 25739. Born: Slane, 2 October 1896. Son of Christopher and Emily Nulty, *née* Mullen, Slane Village. Mother's occupation: Professor of Music. Occupation: Junior Clerk. Enlistment location: Falkirk. Killed in action, France & Flanders, 13 November 1916. Memorial: Pier and Face 16C, Thiepval Memorial. Drogheda War Memorial.

NULTY, Patrick: Private, Leinster Regiment, 2nd Battalion, 4221. Born: Trim. Son of Patrick and Bridget Nulty, The Green, Trim. Father's occupation: Agricultural Labourer, Shepherd. Occupation: Servant. Enlistment location: Drogheda. Served in France from 26 October 1914. Died of wounds, France & Flanders, 6 May 1915. Age: 21. Buried: Newtown, Trim. 'Nulty, Patrick, Private, Leinster Regiment, 2nd Battalion, 4221. 6 May 1915 age 21.' Newtown Cemetery, Trim. 'Nultey, P. Private, Leinster Regiment' (Trim Church of Ireland, Roll of Honour). From the *Meath Chronicle*, 22 May 1915:

Soldiers' Funerals in Trim – A Contrast

During the week the remains of another Trim soldier named Nulty were brought to the town for internment also. Nulty was twice wounded while in action in Flanders whence he was removed to a London hospital, where he succumbed to his wounds. His remains were brought to Trim by his friends.

O

O'BRIEN, Christopher Owen: Rifleman, Rifle Brigade, 4th Battalion, Z/1975. Baptised: Moynalty, 17 February 1894. Son of Michael and Bridget O'Brien, née Clarke, Screebogue, Moynalty. Father's occupation: Farmer. Enlisted 1 September 1914. Enlistment location: Birmingham. Height: 5 foot 6 inches. Hair: Brown. Occupation: (1911) Shop Assistant, (at enlistment) Rubber Worker. Served in France from 18 February 1915. Killed in action, France & Flanders, 8 March 1915. Age: 22. Memorial: II.D.20, Voormezeele Enclosures No. 1 and No. 2.

O'BRIEN, Gerald: Private, Royal Dublin Fusiliers, 10th Battalion, 25125. Baptised: Trim, 14 August 1894. Son of Daniel and Winifred O'Brien, née Dwyer, Trim and later of 25 Armstrong Street, Harold's Cross, Dublin. Killed in action, France & Flanders, 28 May 1917. Age: 22. Memorial: I.K.14, Bailleul Road East Cemetery, St Laurent-Blangy.

O'BRIEN, Joseph: Private, South Lancashire Regiment, 6th Battalion, 300. Baptised: Navan, 14 August 1882. Son of Thomas and Bridget O'Brien, née Quinn, The Factory, Johnstown. Enlisted: 10 July 1908, aged 24. Enlistment location: Warrington, Lancashire. Height: 5 foot 8 inches. Eyes: Grey. Hair: Brown. Having served his six-year term, he re-engaged for a further period of four years in July 1914. Served in France from 8 October to December 1914 and was despatched to the Mediterranean front in August 1915. He embarked at Port Said in February 1916 and landed in Basra on 1 March. Killed in action, Mesopotamia 5 April 1916. Memorial: Panel 23, Basra Memorial.

O'BRIEN, Owen: Private, Leinster Regiment, 2nd Battalion, 330. Born: Moynalty. Son of Mrs Katherine O'Brien, Oakley Park, Kells. Enlistment location: Inverkeithing, Fife. Served in the Balkans. Killed in action, France & Flanders, 11 August 1916. Memorial: Pier and Face 16 C, Thiepval Memorial.

O'CONNOR, J.: From the *Meath Chronicle*, 18 March 1916, 'Intelligence reached Navan during the week of the death in action of Privates Stanislaus Cahill and J. O'Connor, of Navan. Cahill was in the Leinster Regiment and transferred to the Connaught Rangers, and was a native of Navan.'

O'CONNOR, P.: Royal Dublin Fusiliers. 3rd Battalion, Native of Navan. Killed by shrapnel 3 December 1915. (Horneck)

O'DARE, James: Private, Royal Irish Regiment, 2nd Battalion, 6257. Formerly Royal Dublin Fusiliers, 26318. Baptised: Trim, 2 May 1899. Son of James and Bridget O'Dare, *née* Melady, Emmet Street, Trim. Father's occupation: General Labourer. Enlistment location: Athboy. Killed in action, France & Flanders, 21 August 1918. Age: 19. Memorial: II.J.9, Adanac Military Cemetery, Miraumont. James joined under age. His mother got him out but he rejoined. He was wounded in the leg and the stretcher bearers were taking him away when a large shell killed them all. His mother knew he was dead before the telegram came. She told her husband that James was dead, she had seen his face at the window. The telegram arrived shortly after. His uncle, John O'Dare,

James O'Dare.

died as a result of being gassed. James O'Dare joined up at the time of his uncle's death. 'O'Dare, Jas. Private R.I. Regt' (Trim Church of Ireland, Roll of Honour). From the *Meath Chronicle*, 18 March 1916, 'Recruits from Trim and District. Edward Casey, a native of Kilkenny, enlisted in the Royal Irish Fusiliers and James O'Dare, Emmet Street, Trim, the 5th bat. Leinster Regiment.'

O'DARE, John: Sergeant, Leinster Regiment, 6th Battalion, 771. Enlisted in the Leinster regiment, Navan in 1892, aged 19. Served as a private in the Leinster regiment 2nd Battalion for twelve years, until 12 August 1904. Served in South Africa 1901-2. Having left the army he became a Labourer. Husband of Mary Ann O'Dare, *née* Weldon, High Street, Trim. They were married at Trim 1 September 1912. They had a daughter, Mary Bridget. As a member of the reserves he re-enlisted at Navan, 19th August 1914. Aged 41. Height: 5 foot 6 inches. Complexion: Sallow. Eyes: Blue. Hair: Brown. Promoted to Corporal on 3 September 1914 and Sergeant on 2 November 1914. Invalided and wounded, was at Suvla Bay. He was discharged as physically unfit for war service on 25 January 1916. His discharge papers said he was of very good military character, smart, intelligent and hardworking. His illness was described as phthisis which originated in the Dardanelles in 1915. He stated he had been well up to

John O'Dare.

Hospital, Trim, after an illness of a couple of months' duration. The deceased, who was in the prime of his life, was a reserve man and joined his regiment at the outbreak of the war. He was rapidly promoted and took part in the action at Suvla Bay, where he was gassed. He spent some months in an English hospital and was eventually invalided out of the army, receiving a pension. The funeral took place on Friday and was well attended, but there was no military display. Fr. Murphy officiated. RIP.

On the same page of the *Meath Chronicle* is an article recording the enlistment of his nephew, James O'Dare, who was also killed in the war.

September 1915, when he was at Anzac. He contracted dysentery and was sent home. He then developed pleurs-pneumonia. On examination TB was found in the sputum. Date of death: 8 March 1916. Memorial: North of West ruin, Newtown Cemetery, Trim. Newtown Cemetery – '771 Serjeant J. O'Dare, Leinster Regiment 8th March 1916'. From the *Meath Chronicle*, 18 March 1916:

Trim Soldier's Death
On Ash Wednesday John O'Dare, a sergeant of the Leinster Regiment, passed away at the Workhouse

O'KEEFFE, Christopher: Rifleman, Royal Irish Rifles, 7th Battalion, 4683. Baptised: Navan, 1 December 1886. Son of Dan and Mary O'Keeffe, *née* King, Keapock's Lane, later of Infirmary Hill and later of 23 Patrick's Terrace, Navan. Father's occupation: Labourer. Husband of Bridget O'Keeffe, 7 Patricks Terrace, Navan. Occupation: (1911) Drawer for Looms Wool. Enlistment location: Navan. Served in France from 21 December 1915. Killed in action, France & Flanders, 7 September 1916. Memorial: Pier and Face 15A and 15B, Thiepval Memorial.

O'KEEFFE, Joseph Richard: Second Lieutenant, Loyal North Lancashire Regiment, 10th Battalion. Baptised: Duleek, 20 July 1887. Son of William J. and Cathleen O'Keeffe, *née* Ball. Father's occupation: Doctor. In 1901 a student at St Finian's Academy, Navan. In 1911 a medical student living with relatives at Rathmullen, Drogheda. Killed in action, France & Flanders, 4 May 1916. Memorial: II.B.2, Bienvillers Military Cemetery.

O'NEILL, Christopher: Sergeant, Royal Field Artillery, D Battery, 102nd Brigade, 32875. Baptised: Navan, 19 June 1882. Son of James and Kate O'Neill, *née* Smyth, Commons, Navan and later of 8 O'Growney Terrace, Navan. Father's occupation: General Labourer. Enlistment location: Belfast. Served in France from 25 August 1915. Killed in action, France & Flanders, 12 August 1917. Age: 30. Memorial: I.F.27, La Clytte Military Cemetery.

O'NEILL, Patrick: Private, Irish Guards, 2nd Battalion, 10562. Baptised: Dunboyne, 17 February 1885. Son of Patrick and Bridget O'Neill, *née* Hynes, Priestown, Dunboyne. Father's occupation: Labourer. Enlistment location: Drogheda. Killed in action, France & Flanders, 27 June 1917. Age: 32. Memorial: 3.F.16, Ferme-Olivier Cemetery.

O'NEILL, Thomas: Lieutenant, Cavalry Reserve, 2nd Battalion, Attached to 1st/1st Dorset Yeomanry. Son of John and Mary H. O'Neill, Tubride, Oldcastle. Father's occupation: Farmer and Petty Sessions Clerk. Occupation: Farmer's son. Brother of W. O'Neill, Millbrook, Oldcastle. Died of illness contracted on active service with Egyptian Expeditionary Force, King George V Hospital, Dublin, 29 May 1919. Memorial: Loughcrew Church of Ireland Churchyard. 'Lieut. Thomas O'Neill 1st Dorset Yeo' (First World War Memorial, St Kieran's church, Loughcrew).

O'REILLY, Hugh: Private, Royal Scots Fusiliers, 6th/7th Battalion, 24387. Born: Kilmainham, Co. Meath. Son of Philip and Maryanne O'Reilly, Aghamore, Kilmainhamwood. Father's occupation: Railway Labourer. Husband of Sarah O'Reilly, *née* Mackin, 46 Dover Street, Anderston, Glasgow. Date and place of marriage: 22 July 1914, St Patrick's, North Street, Glasgow. Occupation: Spirit Salesman. Enlisted: 9 December 1915. Enlistment location: Glasgow. Age at enlistment: 30 years. Height: 5 foot 7¾ inches. Served in France from September 1916 to December 1916 and from 10 June 1917 until his death. Killed in action, France & Flanders, 22 August 1917. His personal effects included an index book, wallet, crucifix, letters and a photo. Memorial: Panel 60 to 61, Tyne Cot Memorial.

O'REILLY, William: Lance-Sergeant, Royal Irish Fusiliers, 1st Battalion, 9190. Formerly 191, Royal Highlanders. Born: Kingscourt. Residence: Kingscourt. Enlistment location: Edinburgh. Served in France from 22 August 1914. Died at home, 6 January 1917. Memorial: Kilmainhamwood Old Graveyard.

O'ROURKE, Christopher: Private, West Yorkshire Regiment, 2nd Battalion, 9525. Born: Navan. Served in France from 5 November 1914. Killed in action, France & Flanders, 19 December 1914. Memorial: II.K.39, Bailleul Road East Cemetery, St Laurent-Blangy.

OSBORNE, Geoffrey William: Second Lieutenant, Royal Air Force, 7th Sqdn. Baptised Julianstown, 25 February 1893. Son of Francis Charles and Anne Sarah Osborne, Smithstown, Drogheda and later of 82 Vincent Square, Westminster, London. Father's occupation: Gentleman Farmer. Killed in action, France & Flanders, 29 June 1918. Age: 26. Memorial: V.C.28, Longuenesse (St Omer) Souvenir Cemetery. Geoffrey William Osbourne, 2nd Lieut., Royal Air Force, youngest son of Francis Charles Osbourne of Smithstown killed in action 29 June 1918 aged twenty-six years buried in the Souvenir cemetery Lougueverse, St Omer' (Julianstown Church).

OSBORNE, Marcus Stuart: Lieutenant, King's Royal Irish Hussars, 8th Battalion, Secondary Unit: Machine Gun Corps (Infantry) attached 8th Battalion. Born: Balrath. Son of F.D. Osborne, Rosnaree, Slane. Served in France from 3 April 1918. Killed in action, 24 April 1918. Memorial: Panel 3-4, Pozieres Memorial. Drogheda War Memorial.

O'TOOLE, James: Private, Royal Dublin Fusiliers, 9th Battalion, 28040. Born: Ratoath. Residence: Ratoath. Enlistment location: Dublin. Died: France & Flanders, 18 October 1917. Memorial: XII.I.6, Dozinghem Military Cemetery.

OWENS, William: Second Lieutenant. Royal Irish Rifles, 7th Battalion. Son of Patrick Owens, Harristown, Hayes, Navan. Father's occupation: Farmer. Killed in action, France & Flanders, 16 August 1917. Age: 30. Memorial: Panel 138 to 140 and 162 to 162A and 163A, Tyne Cot Memorial.

P

PAGE, Henry George: Pantryman, Mercantile Marine, SS *Marquette*, West Hartlepool. Born Co. Meath. Son of James and Helena Page. Husband of Clara Page, *née* Mitchell, 18 Inglemere Road, Rock Ferry, Birkenhead. Drowned as a result of an attack by an enemy submarine, 23 October 1915. Age: 65. Memorial: Tower Hill Memorial, London.

PALMER, Arthur: Royal Warwickshire Regiment, 14th Battalion, 32562. Formerly 7761 Dragoons. Born: Hackney, London. Son of Thomas and Mary Palmer, 23 Bounces Road, Edmonton, London. Residence: Athboy. Husband of Elizabeth Palmer, Bridge Street, Athboy. Enlistment location: Stratford, Essex. Killed in action, France & Flanders, 26 October 1917. Age: 28. Memorial: Panel 23 to 28 and 163A, Tyne Cot Memorial.

PETTIGRUE, Thomas Percival: Private, Canadian Infantry, British Columbia Regiment, 7th Battalion, 17158. Born: 5 May 1889. Son of Thomas and Elizabeth Pettigrue, White Quarry, Ardbraccan, Navan. Father's occupation: Limestone Contractor. Occupation: Clerk. Enlistment location: 23 September 1914. Height: 5 foot 7½ inches. Complexion: Fair. Eyes: Blue. Hair: Light Brown. Killed in action, France & Flanders, 24 April 1915. Memorial: Panel 18-28-30, Ypres (Menin Gate) Memorial. Percy Pettigrue enlisted in the 1st Canadian contingent and proceeded to France. In the heavy German attack north of Ypres in April 1915 the Canadians repulsed the enemy but suffered heavily. Pettigrue was reported missing and was believed to be dead. From Roll of Honour, Ardbraccan church, now in St Mary's church, Navan, 'Thomas Percy Pettigrue aged 25 years British Columbia Regiment missing Ypres 25 April 1915.'

PHILLIPS, John Paul: Private, South African Infantry, 12th Regiment, 9829. Baptised: Oristown, 30 June 1883. Son of Dr Edward and Mary Angela Phillips, *née* Reilly, Wilkinstown and later 67 Mountjoy Square, Dublin. Father's occupation: General Practioner. Died: Capetown, 10 March 1917. Memorial: Sec. 4. 97451B, Capetown (Maitland) Cemetery.

PHILLIPS, Michael: Private, Leinster Regiment, 2nd Battalion, 3899. Baptised: Navan, 24 April 1893. Son of Michael and Jane Phillips, *née* Lynch, Watergate Street. Father's occupation: General Labourer. Worked in Navan Urban District Council. Residence: Navan. Enlistment location: Navan.

Served in France from 8 February 1915. Killed in action, France & Flanders, 4 March 1915. Memorial: A.13, Ferme Buterne Military Cemetery, Houplines. His son, Michael, also served in 2nd Battalion, Leinster Regiment. From the *Meath Chronicle*, 13 March 1915:

Navan Man Killed at the Front

Mrs Walsh, Navan, has received a letter from the front from her son, Private John Walsh, 2nd Leinster Regiment, dated 6th inst. stating that his uncle, her brother, Michael Phillips, was killed on the 2nd inst. Young Walsh added that he was only ten yards distant from his uncle when he was hit. Private Phillips, who leaves a large family, was an old and respected employee of the Navan Urban Council.

PIERCE, Thomas: Private, South Irish Horse, 1579. Baptised: Navan, 25 July 1891. Son of John and Catherine Pierce, *née* Traynor, Trimgate Street, Navan and later of 6 Hospital Lane, Islandbridge, Dublin. Residence: Dublin. Enlistment location: Dublin. Killed in action, France & Flanders, 22 June 1917. Age: 25. Memorial: XIX.A.7, Loos British Cemetery.

PIGOTT, William Gregor: Rifleman, Royal Irish Rifles, 15th Battalion, 41200. Formerly 4th Hussars, 24620. Baptised: Balrathboyne, Kells, 3 March 1885. Son of George and Mary Pigott, Kells. Father's occupation: Mason. Occupation: Farm Servant. Husband of Maria Alicia Pigott, 3 William Street, Portlaw, Co. Waterford. Residence: Portlaw, Co. Waterford. Enlistment location: Tralee, Co. Kerry.

In Loving Memory
OF
WILLIAM GREGOR PIGOTT
Killed in Action September 18th, 1918.
AGED 33 YEARS.

William Gregor Pigott. (Courtesy of Sandra Pigott)

Killed in action, France & Flanders, 18 September 1918. Age: 33. Memorial: In north-west part, Veldwezelt Communal Cemetery. William Pigott served in the Somme in 1915. Taken prisoner and electrocuted while trying to escape. William entered Allenstown School, Ardbraccan on 25 September 1893 and had attended school in Kells previously. His older brother, Charles Stewart Pigott, served in the Merchant Navy.

PLUNKETT, Hugh: Private, Irish Guards, 2nd Battalion, 10860. Baptised: Ratoath, 12 September 1891. Son of Matthew and Mary Plunkett, née Henry, Crickstown, Ashbourne. Father's occupation: Herdsman. Occupation: Labourer. Enlistment location: Dublin. Killed in action, France & Flanders, 27 November 1917. Age: 27. Memorial: Panel 2 and 3, Cambrai Memorial, Louveral.

POTTER, John: Private, Cheshire Regiment, 13th Battalion, W/65. Baptised: Duleek, 29 December 1892. Son of Thomas and Catherine Potters, née McKeon, Downstown. Father's occupation: Railway Plate Layer. Occupation: General Labourer. Residence: Duleek. Enlistment location: Port Sunlight. Served in France from 25 September 1915. Killed in action, France & Flanders, 7 July 1916. Memorial: Pier and Face 3C and 4A, Thiepval Memorial. Drogheda War Memorial. Diary of Cheshire Regiment, '7th Friday. Over the parapet at 8.5 A.M. After suffering severe casualties we reached our objective and consolidated. A number of prisoners and war material fell into our hands. Casualties on this day very heavy 18 Officers and 243 other ranks.'

POTTERTON, William Hubert: Lieutenant, Royal Engineers, 23rd Field Company. Born: Dublin. Son of William and Kathleen Potterton, Freffans, Trim and Palmerston Park, Dublin. Father's occupation: Cattle Salesmaster. Husband of Adelaide Elizabeth Potterton, née Matthews of Dublin, Northern Bank House, Grafton Street, Dublin. Potterton was an engineer and graduate of Trinity. A brother, Norman, also served in the war and survived. Killed in action, Battle of the Somme, 24 July 1916. Age: 24. Memorial: I.K.29, Albert Communal Cemetery Extension. He is commemorated on the war memorial in Trinity and also on one in Connolly Station – as a member of the staff of the Great Northern Railway. 'Lieut. W. H. Potterton R.E.' (Trim Church of Ireland, Roll of Honour). From the *Meath Chronicle*, 8 January 1916:

Meath Officers Wounded
Three young officers, members of South Meath families, who gallantly responded to the call of duty on the outbreak of war have been wounded but are progress-

ing favourably. They are Second Lieutenant Purdon of the Rifle Brigade; Second Lieutenant W.H. Potterton, Royal Engineers; and Second Lieutenant Fowler, King's Royal Rifles … Lieutenant Potterton is a son of Mr. William Potterton, of Freffans, Trim, the well-known cattle salesmaster. This young officer had a very narrow escape from death in Flanders. A bullet grazed his left breast, but happily did not inflict any very serious injury. He is now recruiting his health in Dublin …

POTTS, Joseph: Gordan Highlanders. Native of Navan. Joined on outbreak of war at Glasgow. Killed in France, March 1916. (Horneck).

PRESTON, Arthur John Dillon: Captain, Royal Dublin Fusiliers, 6th Battalion, Son of Major Arthur and Gertrude Preston, Swainston, Kilmessan. Husband of Sylvia Wyke Preston, Clowbryn, Greystones, Co. Wicklow. Killed in action, 15 August 1915. Age: 29. Mentioned in Despatches. Memorial: Special Memorial 50, Azmak Cemetery, Suvla. His son, John Nathaniel Preston (Nat), was born in January 1915. From *De Ruvigny's Roll of Honour, 1914-1924*, volume 1:

Preston, Arthur John Dillon, Captain 2nd Battalion, Royal Dublin Fusiliers, only son of Major Arthur John Preston, of Swainstown, Co. Meath who was in the Duke of Wellington's Regiment, B.A. Trinity College, Justice of the Peace for Co. Durham and Co. Meath by his wife, Gertrude Mary, daughter of Richard Knight, of Bobbing Court, Co. Kent. Born Luther House, Huddersfield, 16 November 1885. Educated Malvern College. Gazetted 2nd Lieutenant to the 3rd (Militia) Battalion, of the Durham L.I. 5 October 1904. Posted to the 1st Battalion, Dublin Fusiliers, 2nd March 1907. Promoted Lieutenant 15 December 1909 and Captain 2nd Battalion, 7 June 1914. Served with the 1st Battalion, in Egypt where he joined the Mounted Infantry, winning at Cairo the Lloyd Lindsay prize. At the outbreak of the European War he was ordered to Naas and afterwards to the Curragh to raise the 6th Service Battalion, of the Royal Dublin Fusiliers with which he proceeded to the Gallipoli Peninsula on 9 July. He took part in all the heavy fighting at Suvla Bay until 15 August when he fell in the moment of victory. The Colonel of his Battalion, writing to his widow, remarked: "I am sure all Ireland will soon hear of the charge of the Dublins and Munsters on that (15th) afternoon. Your husband (Captain Preston, second in command) was responsible for it and organised it splendidly; and in conjunction with Captain Whyte he brilliantly led it. It was a magnificent sight considering they charged up a hill through a hail of bombs and bullets. Captain Preston got safely on the hill (capturing the trench), but in the counter-attack was fatally wounded in the right breast. I was the last officer to speak to him and told him how splendidly he had done. Personally I feel his death very much. No man could have helped his colonel more than he, the success of the regiment was greatly due to him." Captain White, Royal Dublin Fusiliers, wrote: "We closed on the Munsters, and all collected on some dead ground about 100 yards from the crest; I was sitting beside John, and he was in his usual spirits, laughing and joking. When word came that we were to clear the ridge we fixed bayonets, then we all started together, Dublins and Munsters, John shouting "Come on boys." They (the Turks) threw bombs and opened fire upon us as we neared the top but we went straight on and rushed the trench. The Turks put up their hands. I saw John stop his men who were just going to bayonet a Turkish officer. As you know he was my best friend, and was loved by everyone in the regiment, officers, N.C.O.s and men. The only consolation is that he died a glorious death, lead-

ing his men to victory, the death I am sure he would have chosen." Captain Preston wrote to his wife on that fatal 15 August remarking: "I have had six hours sleep and am back full of buck and life." Also to his father a five-page letter. The battle had even then commenced in the valley below. It was written under strenuous circumstances, no change of clothes for five nights, and only six hours sleep, no chance of a wash, and exposed to the heat of a tropical sun, yet his last written words were: "Love to you all. I am very fit and quite happy." He and the Adjutant, Captain Richards, who fell at the same time, were buried in the same grave close to the sea shore at Suvla Bay. A flat gravestone covers them with their names engraved under the words "In Victory". He was mentioned for the gallant and distinguished service in the field by Sir Ian Hamilton in his despatches of 11 December 1915. While in Egypt he and Lieutenant Cozier sailed some hundred miles up the White Nile from Khartoum, in a rough native boat, on which occasion they secured a fine bag of big game, including lion, buffalo, elephant, hippo and various specimens of antelope, deer, etc. He was a keen sportsman, well known with the Kildare and Meath hounds, a fine cricketer and tennis player, and the best shot with revolver and rifle (tied) in his Battalion. Captain Preston married at St Mary-le-Bone, London, 24 March 1914, Sylvia, daughter of Arthur James Billin, of Tadworth, Co. Surrey, and had a son: John Nathaniel, born 27 January 1915.

PURDON, George Hardress: Second Lieutenant, King's Royal Rifle Corps, 2nd Battalion. Baptised: Trim, 16 January 1897. Son of Colonel Edward Winter and Cecilia Purdon, Tullyard, Trim and later of Lisnabin, Killucan, Co. Westmeath. Trim. Father's occupation: Land Agent. Killed in action, 23 July 1916. Age: 19. Memorial: Pier and Face 13 A and 13 B, Thiepval Memorial. From Trim Church of Ireland, Roll of Honour, 'Purdon, G.H. Second Lieutenant 60th Rifles K.R.R.' From the *Meath Chronicle*, 8 January 1916:

Meath Officers Wounded

Three young officers, members of South Meath families, who gallantly responded to the call of duty on the outbreak of war have been wounded but are progressing favourably. They are Second Lieutenant Purdon of the Rifle Brigade; Second Lieutenant W.H. Potterton, Royal Engineers; and Second Lieutenant Fowler, King's Royal Rifles. Lieutenant Purdon is son of Col. and Mrs Purdon, formerly of Tullyard House, Trim and at one time very energetic members of Trim Rural District Council.

From the *Meath Chronicle*, 19 August 1916, 'The magistrates at Trim Petty Sessions last Saturday passed a resolution of condolence to Col. and Mrs Purdon Winter on the death at the front of their youngest son.'

Q

QUINN, James: Private, Leinster Regiment, 2nd Battalion, 4571. Born: Navan. Enlistment location: Drogheda. Brother of T. Quinn, Royal Irish Rifles, 4526. Served in France from 15 September 1915. Killed in action. France & Flanders. 6 November 1917. Third Battle of Ypres. Memorial: IV.O.6, Roisel Communal Cemetery Extension.

QUINN, Peter: Private, Irish Guards, 2nd Battalion, 6552. Baptised: Trim, 30 September 1895. Son of James and Elizabeth Quinn, *née* Duff, Boardsmill, Trim. Father's occupation: Agricultural Labourer, Miller. Member of Irish National Volunteers. Occupation: Labourer. Enlistment location: Drogheda. Served in France from 17 August 1915. Killed at the Battle of Loos. Killed in action, France & Flanders, 30 September 1915. Age: 20. Memorial: Panel 9 and 10, Loos Memorial. From the *Meath Chronicle*, 22 January 1916, 'The parents of Mr. Peter Quinn, who resided at Boardsmill, near Trim, have just received official information from the War Office that their son has fallen in battle. The sad intelligence has caused widespread regret in the district.'

R

RADCLIFFE, Herbert Travers: Captain, Leinster Regiment, 5th Battalion. Baptised: Kells, 11 August 1882. Son of George Edward and Emma Mary Alexandria Radcliff, Headfort Place, Kells and later of Wilmount, Kells. Father's occupation: Gentleman Farmer. Occupation: Lieutenant on Reserve List, Farmer, Clerk of the Petty Sessions. Killed in action, France & Flanders, 15 March 1915. Age: 32. Memorial: Ypres (Menin Gate) Memorial. From Julianstown church, stained-glass window, 'Herbert Travers Radcliffe, Captain Leinster Regiment killed in action at St Eloi 15th March 1915.' From the War Memorial, 1914-1918, Kells Church of Ireland, 'Captain H.T. Radcliffe, Leinster Regiment.' From the *Meath Chronicle*, 20 March 1915:

Captain Radcliffe Killed at the Front
We regret to learn that a telegram reached Kells yesterday announcing that Captain Reginald T. Radcliffe of the Leinster Regiment has been killed in action. Captain Radcliffe was the son of the late Mr. George Radcliffe of Wilmount, Kells and had held for some years the office of Clerk of Petty Sessions for Kells, Moynalty and George's Cross. The deepest sympathy will be felt for his bereaved relatives.

From the *Meath Chronicle*, 27 March 1915:

The Late Captain Radcliffe –
How he met his death
The following letters, telling how the late Captain Herbert Travers Radcliffe met his death, have come to his mother, Mrs Radcliffe of Wilmount. The event is widely lamented in the district of Kells. Everyone who knew the Captain speaks of him as a straightforward and kindly man. Among every class there is a feeling of deep sympathy for his afflicted mother and other relatives.

17th March 1915
Dear Mrs Radcliffe – It is with the deepest sympathy and regret that I have to inform you that your son was killed early on the morning of the 15th. He was holding a trench which had a garrison of 30 men and which was attacked by 100 Germans at or soon after dawn. He was killed instantaneously by a bullet which struck his head, and could have suffered no pain. I may add that the Germans were beaten off with a loss of 34 killed alone. During the few days he had been

with us he proved himself a brave and gallant officer, and we deplore the loss of a good comrade and offer you a whole-hearted sympathy. His personal belongings I am having collected and forwarded to you as soon as possible. The place where your son was killed is called St Eloi about two miles south of Ypres – Believe me.

Yours very truly

A.B. Prowse

Lieut-Col Commanding 1st Leinster Regiment.

17th March 1915

Dear Mrs Radcliffe – A few lines to express my deepest sympathy on the death of Herbert, and to enclose a few letters which came to him afterwards. I was with him when he was killed. He was my company commander both here and in Passage and like all the men of the company I would have done anything for him. He always thought of the men first and afterwards himself and it was through his unselfishness that he met his death. Someone said the Germans were leaving their trench to attack and no one looked out so he looked over and was hit. He suffered no pain whatever. He was buried on Monday night and we have handed his things to the Quartermaster, who will send them on to you in a few weeks. I only knew too well how useless it is to express sympathy, but I have taken this opportunity of expressing, not only my known sympathy but that of all the men of the company, who had grown to love him, even in a few days under his command – I am yours very sincerely C.J. Mackay (Lieut.).

From *De Ruvigny's Roll of Honour, 1914-1924*, volume 1:

Radcliffe, Herbert Travers. Captain 5th Reserve, attached 1st Battalion, Leinster Regiment. Second son of the late George Edward Radcliff of Wilmount, Kells, Co. Meath by his wife, Emma May Alexandria, daughter of John Travers Madden, of Inch House, Balbriggan. Born: Kells, 11 August 1882. Educated: Royal School, Armagh. Gazetted 2nd Lieutenant, Leinster Regiment, 27 October 1906; promoted Lieutenant and Captain 10 February 1913. Went to France 6 March 1915, attached to the 1st Battalion, and was killed in action at St Eloi, 15 March following. Unmarried.

RAFFERTY, Patrick: Private, Royal Dublin Fusiliers, 6th Battalion, 12588. Born: Dunshaughlin. Residence: Dundalk, Co. Louth. Enlistment location: St Helens. Served in Balkans from 7 August 1915. Killed in action, Gallipoli, 9 August 1915. Memorial: Panel 190 to 196, Helles Memorial.

REGAN, Matthew J.: Rifleman, Royal Irish Rifles, 7th Battalion, 3875. Baptised: Trim, 10 September 1894. Son of Michael and Catherine Regan, *née* Darby, Castle Street, Trim and later of Effernock, Trim. Father's occupation: Shoemaker. Occupation: Apprentice to Coach Building. Residence: Trim. Enlistment location: Drogheda. Died at home, 5 May 1915. Age: 20. Memorial: Newtown Cemetery, Trim. Newtown Cemetery, Trim, 'Regan, M.J. Quis separavit 3875 Rifleman M.J. Regan, Royal Irish Rifles, 5 May 1915 age 20. From the *Meath Chronicle*, 22 May 1915:

> Soldiers' Funerals in Trim – A Contrast
> On Saturday the 8th inst. the remains of a soldier named Regan belonging to one of the Leinster regiments and a native of Trim were removed from an hospital in Cork City to Trim for interment. The deceased was buried with full military honours. A cordon of soldiers from his Battalion bore the coffin to the graveside and a salute fired over the grave. Regan had only been three months in training when he contracted pneumonia. Shortly after his removal to Cork he expired.

REGAN, Patrick: Royal Navy. Trim district. Killed. (Horneck)

REGAN, Paul: Sergeant, Irish Guards, 6651. Baptised: Beauparc, 5 March 1897. Son of Thomas and Catherine Regan, *née* Kelly, Curraghtown, Brownstown, Navan. Father's occupation: Caretaker. Died: 30 January 1919. Buried: Plot A. 189, Navan New Cemetery.

REILLY, James: Private, Leinster Regiment, 2nd Battalion, 4100. Baptised: Trim, 16 April 1893. Son of Thomas and Anne Reilly, *née* Hughes, Dogstown, Trim. Father's occupation: Agricultural Labourer. Served in France from 6 December 1914. Died at home, 12 January 1918. Age: 26. Memorial: Moymet Old Graveyard, Trim.

REILLY, J.: Private, Leinster Regiment (Trim Church of Ireland, Roll of Honour).

REILLY, James: Driver, Royal Field Artillery, A Battery, 91st Brigade, 25013. Born: Navan. Son of Bernard and Kate Reilly. Brother of Annie Mathews, 4 Echlin Street, Dublin. Occupation: Labourer and Groom. Worked for two years before enlistment as general farm labourer with Mr Gormell, Corporation Street, Bolton, England. Residence: Manchester. Enlisted: 2 September 1914. Enlistment location: Manchester. Height: 5 foot 5½ inches. Complexion: Fresh. Eyes: Brown. Hair: Black. Served in France from 21 July 1915. Fell ill, France, December 1916. Transferred to England December 1916. Discharged, ill with dysentery, 16 October 1917. Died: King George V Hospital, Dublin, 24 November 1917. Age: 35. Memorial: Teltown Graveyard. '25013 Driver J. Reilly Royal Field Artillery, died 24 November 1917 aged 35 years' (Teltown Graveyard).

REILLY, James: Private, Royal Irish Fusiliers, 7th Battalion, 23156. Born: Moynalty. Residence: Mullagh, Co. Cavan. Enlistment location: Cavan. Killed in action, France & Flanders, 2 June 1916. Memorial: I.N.3, St Patrick's Cemetery, Loos.

REILLY, John: Rifleman, Royal Irish Rifles, 2nd Battalion, 7689. Baptised Navan, 4 February 1889. Son of Peter and Alice Reilly, *née* Downs, Brews Hill, Navan and later of 8 Middle Gardiners Street, Dublin. Enlistment location: Dublin. Served in France from 15 August 1914. Killed in action, France & Flanders, 27 October 1914. Age: 25. Memorial: Panel 42 and 43, Le Touret Memorial.

REILLY, John: Private, Argyll and Sutherland Highlanders, 2nd Battalion, 9080. Born: Kells. Residence: Glasgow. Enlistment location: Paisley, Renfrews. John Reilly appeared in a regimental magazine, noted as having come to the 2nd Battalion, on the 11 January 1905 with a draft of men from England and taken on E company strength and received his first good conduct badge in February 1906. Served in France from 10 August 1914. Killed in action, France & Flanders, 10 November 1914. Memorial: Panel 9 and 10, Ploegsteert Memorial.

A letter returned to Mr. Sludden, Allandale, Castlecary, on Friday of last week, seems to bear out the story circulated some months ago that Pte. John Reilley, a reservist who went out with the Argyll and Sutherland Highlanders had been killed in action. A post card received by Mrs Godley from one of her sons, with whom Reilley at one time lodged, bore the words "Big Paddy is killed". Reilley, who

John Reilly.

was a kilnsetter at Messrs Stein's Works, was popularly known as "Big Paddy." Reilley had latterly been staying with Mr. Sludden, who sent a letter addressed to him. The letter was returned by the authorities and across it was written "Missing" also "Killed at Mons". Reilley was 33 years of age and unmarried. He was through the South African War." Newspaper report courtesy of the Argyll and Sutherland Highlander Museum, Stirling Castle, Scotland. (The mention of the Battle of Mons is either incorrect or this article may refer to a different John Reilly.)

REILLY, John: Private, Irish Guards, 1st Battalion, 11007. Baptised Rathmolyon, 27 July 1888. Son of Thomas and Elizabeth Reilly, née Magrath, Jordanstown. Enlistment location: Trim. Died of wounds, France & Flanders, 9 October 1917. Age: 29. Memorial: Panel 10 to 11, Tyne Cot Memorial.

REILLY, John: Lance-Sergeant, Guards Machine Gun Regiment, 4th Battalion, 1177. With the Irish Guards, 4359, until 1 February 1917. Baptised Oristown, 20 October 1895. Son of Matthew and Margaret Reilly, née McDermott, Randlestown, Navan. Residence: Randlestown, Navan. Enlistment location: Drogheda. Served in France from 13 August 1914. Died of wounds, 25 April 1918. Age:

21. Memorial: XVII.B.4, Bienvillers Military Cemetery.

REILLY, Michael: Private, Leinster Regiment, 2nd Battalion, 3150. Born: Killincare, Co. Meath. Son of Matthew and Elizabeth Reilly, Clugga, Mullagh, Kells. Enlistment location: Drogheda. Served in Balkans from 9 July 1915. Killed in action, France & Flanders, 12 April 1917. Age: 38. Memorial: Bay 9, Arras Memorial.

REILLY, Michael: Fireman and Trimmer, Mercantile Marine, SS *Clover*, London. Born Co. Meath. Son of William and Rose Reilly. Husband of Rose Reilly, née Creaney, 36 Gordon Street, Belfast. Drowned as a result of an attack by an enemy submarine, 19 October 1917. Age: 40. Memorial: Tower Hill Memorial, London.

REILLY, Patrick: Private, Irish Guards, 2nd Battalion, 8624. Baptised Navan, 26 September 1898. Son of Thomas and Catherine Reilly, née Dunclas, Kilcarn and later of 6 St Finian's Terrace, Navan. Occupation: Messenger Post Office. Enlistment location: Drogheda. Killed in action, France & Flanders, 13 September 1916. Age: 18. Memorial: Pier and Face 7D, Thiepval Memorial.

REILLY, Patrick: Rifleman, London Regiment Queen Victoria's Rifles, 1st/9th Battalion, 393629. Formerly

5058, 8th London Regiment. Baptised Navan, 3 November 1897. Son of the Mathew and Mary Anne Reilly, née Duglas, Kilcarne, Navan. Father's occupation: Blacksmith. Residence: Navan. Enlistment location: Navan. Killed in action, France & Flanders, 14 April 1917. Age: 19. Memorial: Bay 10, Arras Memorial.

REILLY, Patrick: Private, Royal Irish Regiment, 7th Battalion, 25732. Formerly South Irish Horse, 2409. Born: Athboy. Enlistment location: Athboy. Son of the Edward and Mary Reilly. Killed in action, France & Flanders, 21 March 1918. Age: 25. Memorial: Panel 30 and 31, Pozieres Memorial.

REILLY, Thomas: Private, Leinster Regiment, 7th Battalion, A Company, 387. Born: Kells. Son of Mary Reilly, Carrick Street, Kells. Enlistment location: Drogheda. Served in France from 17 December 1915. Killed in action, France & Flanders, 3 September 1916. Age: 33. Memorial: Pier and Face 16C, Thiepval Memorial.

REILLY, William: Private, Royal Inniskilling Fusiliers, 9th Battalion, 28007. Baptised Ardbraccan, 28 October 1889. Son of Thomas and Rebecca Reilly, White Quarry, Ardbraccan. Husband of Elizabeth Reilly, 'Milverton', Greystones, Co. Wicklow. Father's occupation: Stone Cutter. Occupation: Stone Cutter.

Enlistment location: Navan. Killed in action, France & Flanders, 15 October 1918. Memorial: III.C.18, Dadizeele New British Cemetery. From Roll of Honour, Ardbraccan church, now in St Mary's church, Navan, 'William Reilly aged 28 years Royal Inniskilling Fusiliers killed in action at Hulse 15 October 1918.'

REILLY, William: Sergeant, Irish Guards, 1st Battalion, 2635. Baptised: Lobinstown, 25 February 1883. Son of Patrick and Ellen Reilly, née Murphy. Husband of Helen Kathleen Reilly, 37 Cassella Road, New Cross, London. Enlistment location: Dublin. Served in France from 13 September 1914. Killed in action, France & Flanders, 4 August 1917. Age: 34. Memorial: IV.A.16, Artillery Woods Cemetery.

RENNICKS, Richard: Private, Leinster Regiment, 7th Battalion, 5394. Formerly Royal Inniskilling Fusiliers, 28008. Baptised: Ardbraccan, 30 April 1894. Son of Bernard and Jane Rennicks, White Quarry, Ardbraccan. Twin to Margaret. Father's occupation: Stone Cutter. Occupation: Stone Cutter. Enlistment location: Navan. Died of wounds, France & Flanders, 8 March 1917. Memorial: I.C.24, Loker Churchyard. 'Richard Rennicks aged 22 years 7th Leinster Regiment killed in action near Locre 8 March 1917' (Roll of Honour, Ardbraccan Church, now in St Mary's Church Navan). From the *Meath Chronicle*, 2 October 1915: 'Six young men from Ardbraccan, named Joe Lynch, Wm. Rennicks, Road. Rennicks, Wm Reilly have joined the Inniskilling Fusiliers. They formerly belonged to Ardbraccan Corps, I.N.V.. From the *Meath Chronicle*, 31 March 1917

> Intelligence of the death from wounds of Pte. R. Rennicks reached Ardbraccan last week. He was a universal favourite and was nine months in France. He was being conveyed on the back of a comrade named Masterson out of the firing line when death ensued. The deceased whose death is deeply regretted was a member of Bohermeen Football Club.

RENNIX, John: Irish Guards. Duleek district. Killed. (Horneck)

REYNOLDS, Frederick: Seaman, Royal Naval Reserve, HMS *Monmouth*, 3241A. Baptised: St Mary's, Drogheda, 20 July 1891. Son of Thomas and Mary Reynolds, *née* Ward, Mornington. Father's occupation: Fisherman and Pilot. Killed in action at the Battle of Coronel, 1 November 1914. Memorial: 6, Portsmouth Naval Memorial, Hampshire. Drogheda War Memorial. From *Drogheda Independent*, 28 November 1914:

> Deep sympathy is felt with Thomas Reynolds of Mornington, and his wife on the loss of their youngest

son, Fred, who was on the HMS *Monmouth* when the ship was sunk in the Pacific during an engagement with a German flotilla. Deceased was a promising young man, and had only attained his 22nd year. He was highly respected and esteemed by all who knew him and much sympathy is expressed for his parents in their sorrow and bereavement.

REYNOLDS, Laurence: Seaman, Royal Naval Reserve, HMS *Laurentic*, 4554B. Baptised: St Mary's, Drogheda, 12 February 1883. Son of James and Mary Reynolds, *née* Carroll, Mornington, Drogheda. Father's occupation: General Labourer, Fisherman. Occupation: (1901) Fisherman and Agricultural Labourer, (1911), Fisherman. Husband of Anna Reynolds, 17 Marsh Road, Drogheda. Married: 14 December 1916. Killed in mine explosion off north Irish coast, 25 January 1917. Age 33. Memorial: 27, Portsmouth Naval Memorial. Drogheda War Memorial.

REYNOLDS, Peter: Private, Royal Dublin Fusiliers, 8th Battalion, 19835. Born: Clonfane, Trim. Son of Daniel Reynolds. Father's occupation: Agricultural Labourer. Husband of Mrs E. Reynolds, later Chisnall, 103 Leigh Street, Earlestown, Lancashire. Killed in action, France & Flanders, 1 February 1917. Memorial: I.A.6, La Laiterie Military Cemetery.

ROBINSON, Charles: Corporal, Royal Inniskilling Fusiliers, C Company, 7th Battalion, 19579. Born Summerhill. Son of William and Hannah Robinson, née Sarson. Residence: Court Devenish, Athlone, Co. Westmeath. Enlistment location: Ballinasloe. Killed in action, France & Flanders, 16 August 1917. Age: 21. Memorial: Panel 70 to 72 Tyne Cot Memorial.

ROCHFORD, Joseph: Lance-Corporal, Queen's Own Hussars, 4th Battalion, 10873. Baptised: Trim, 13 May 1894. Son of Bernard and Catherine Rochford, née Larkin, Newhaggard, Trim. Father's occupation: Farmer. Brother, Michael, also killed in the war. A third brother, Peter, survived the war. Enlistment location: Drogheda. Served in France from 15 August 1914. Died of wounds, France & Flanders, 5 November 1914. Award: 1914 Star. Memorial: B.19, Bailleul Communal Cemetery (Nord). Rochford, Joseph, Trooper 5th RI Lancers (Trim Church of Ireland, Roll of Honour). Family source said he was captured and made a prisoner of war. He was not able to march and a German officer shot him in the head.

ROCHFORD, Michael: Private, Leinster Regiment, 2nd Battalion, 10084. Baptised: Trim, 29 July 1897. Son of Bernard and Catherine Rochford, née Larkin, Newhaggard, Trim. Father's occupation: Farmer.

Brother, Joseph, also killed in the war. A third brother, Peter, survived the war. Enlistment location: Drogheda. Served in France from 8 September 1914. Killed in action, France & Flanders, 20 October 1914. First battle of the 2nd Battalion, took place 18-20 October 1914 at Armentieres. Memorial: Panel 10, Ploesteert Memorial. From Trim Church of Ireland, Roll of Honour, 'Rochford, M. Private, Leinster Regiment.' Family source said he died during field surgery when they were taking his leg off.

ROE, Joseph: Private, Irish Guards, 1st Battalion, 10534. Baptised Trim, 21 July 1897. Son of Patrick and Elizabeth Roe, née Kelly, High Street, Trim. Father's occupation: Publican. Enlistment location: Dublin. Died of wounds, France & Flanders, 24 August 1916 or 23 August 1918. Age: 21. Memorial H.19, St Hilaire Cemetery Extension, Frevent.

ROGERS, Christopher: Acting Fitter Sergeant, Royal Field Artillery, 29th Battery, 22862. Born: Dublin. Son of Abraham Rogers. Husband of Agnes Rogers, 17 O'Growney Terrace, Navan. Enlistment location: Dublin. Served in France from 19 August 1914. Killed in action, France & Flanders, 27 March 1916. Age: 33. Memorial: I.8, Dickebisch New Military Cemetery. From the *Meath Chronicle*, 13 May 1916, 'Sergt. Rogers, Royal Field Artillery, belonging to Navan, was killed at the front on March 27th. He was recommended for the D.C.M. He leaves a widow and family.'

ROGERS, James: Private, Irish Guards, 2nd Battalion, 4265. Born: Drumree. Enlistment location: Dublin. Served in France from 13 August 1914. Killed in action, France & Flanders, 27 September 1915. Memorial: Panel 9 and 10, Loos Memorial.

ROGERS, James: Lance-Corporal, Labour Corps, 12th Labour Battalion, 711th Company, 348319. Formerly Royal Engineers, 163200. Born: Trim. Enlistment location: Dublin. Died: Salonica, 19 September 1917. Memorial: 10, Kirechkoi-Hortakoi Military Cemetery.

ROURKE, John: Rifleman, Royal Irish Rifles, 2nd Battalion, 7253. Born: Co. Meath. Son of Andrew and Sarah Rourke, 99 North Strand Road, Dublin. Husband of Mary Rourke, 17 Ballybough Cottages, Dublin. Enlistment location: Dublin. Served in France from 21 August 1914. Killed in action, France & Flanders, 26 October 1914. Age: 30. Memorial: Panel 42 and 43, Le Touret Memorial.

ROURKE, John: Private, Connaught Rangers, 2nd Battalion, 10622. Baptised: Rathmolyon/Enfield, 21 September 1895. Son of John and Anne Rourke, née Allen, Rathcore, Enfield. Father's occupation: Farm Labourer. Enlistment location: Naas, Co. Kildare. Served in France from 14 August 1914. Killed in action, France & Flanders, 1 November 1914. Age: 19. Memorial: LII.F.11, Poelcapelle British Cemetery.

ROWLEY, The Hon. George Cecil: Second Lieutenant, King's Royal Rifle Corps, 5th Battalion attached 1st Battalion. Son of Hercules Edward Rowley, fourth Baron Langford of Summerhill and his wife Georgina Mary, daughter of Sir Richard Sutton. Killed in action, 17 February 1917. Age: 20. Memorial: I.E.17, Regina Trench Cemetery, Grandcourt. Memorial Agher church, 'In memory of Hon.ble George Cecil Rowley 2nd Lieutenant King's Royal Rifle Corps. Son of the 4th Baron Langford killed in action near Miraunmont 17th Feb. 1917 aged 20. Buried near Miraunmont.' Trim Church of Ireland, Roll of Honour, '2nd Lt. Hon G.C. Rowley Second Lieutenant 60th Rifles K.R.R.'

RUSSELL, Andrew Joseph: Sergeant, London Regiment, Royal Fusiliers, 4th Battalion, 3046. Baptised: Kells, 18 September 1887. Son of Patrick and Mary Russell, née Doyle, Church Street, Kells. Father's occupation: Professor of Music. Residence: Highgate. Enlistment location: Shaftesbury Street. Served in Egypt from 24 August 1915. Killed in action, France & Flanders, 14 September 1916 Age: 29: Memorial: X.D.9A, Etaples

Military Cemetery. From the *Meath Chronicle*, 23 September 1916:

Kells Man Fatally Wounded in France
We regret to learn that Mr. Andrew J. Russell, B.A. a native of Kells, has died of wounds received in the recent hard fighting on the Somme front in France. The news that reached Kells last Friday lacked official confirmation, and it was hoped that it might prove unfounded, as other such stories have sometimes proven, but unfortunately later advices from semi-official sources show that the sad tidings were only too true. A telegram received on Tuesday states that he died in France on Thursday 14th September of wounds received on the previous Sunday. Many friends in various districts and the people of his native place have learned with much regret of poor "Andy's" early demise. He was aged about 25 years. He was the second son of the late Mr. Patrick Russell, some time organist of St Columbkille's Church, Kells. He was educated in the Christian Brothers' Schools, Kells, and showed ability of a high order, especially in mathematical subjects. He followed up a series of brilliant successes in the Intermediate exams by taking out the B.A. degree of the National University. Shortly before commencement of the war he was awarded a scholarship by the Department of Technical Instruction enabling him to take a course of special study at the London School of Economics. While pursuing his studies in London, he with a number of fellow-students, enlisted in a British regiment. Having served at Malta and Salonica, he was sometime this year transferred to the more dangerous sphere of action in France. "Andy" inherited some of his father's musical talents. He possessed a fine baritone voice, and was much in request by organisers of local concerts. At one time he took an active part in organising Gaelic sports and was an expert wielder of the caman. He was amongst the most enthusiastic of the Kells Volunteers, and evincing a marked taste for military pursuits, and with his love of adventure, it was not surprising that he should have embraced the opportunity of learning the soldier's trade. R.I.P.".

From the *Meath Chronicle*, 30 September 1916:

How Sergeant Russell Died – Chaplain's Sad Message.
The Rev. Fr. McCabe, Roman Catholic Chaplain to the regiment to which the late Sergt. A.J. Russell of Kells belonged, has sent the following letter to

a friend of the deceased:- "Your letter has just reached me, and I hasten to give you all the details in my power concerning Sergt. Russell, your friend. He was seriously wounded in the chest by shrapnel, and though he had the best possible medical attention and nursing, the wound caused his death. He had little or no pain and was quite conscious up to a few hours of the end. I was with him twice – the last time the day previous to his death. He received all the Sacraments of the Church in most edifying dispositions and he offered up his life willingly to God when he knew he was in grave danger. I hope all his friends will be resigned to God's holy will, and to offer it up to God, even as he made the sacrifice of his life, like the gallant soldier and fervent Catholic that he was. It should be of great comfort to his people to know how well he was prepared for the end and how surely the merciful Judge, Our Blessed Lord, will have received his soul. May he rest in peace – I am yours in deep sympathy J.C.A.E. McCabe C.SSR. R.C. chaplain.'

On Monday morning Mass was celebrated in St Columbkille's Church by Rev. Father Casey C.C. for the repose of the soul of the deceased. A number of relatives and friends attended.

RUSSELL, William Francis: Corporal, Royal Dublin Fusiliers, 1st Battalion, 29064. Baptised: Stamullin, 7 February 1899. Son of Robert and Mary Russell, *née* Cantwell, Demanistown, Julianstown. Father's occupation: General Labourer. Enlistment location: Drogheda. Died of wounds, France & Flanders, 14 October 1918. Age: 20. Memorial: VI.A.9, Dadizeele New British Cemetery. Drogheda War Memorial.

RYAN, Hugh Joseph: Private, Royal Dublin Fusiliers, 8th Battalion, 26631. Baptised: Rathmolyon, 22 August 1883. Son of Michael and Anne Ryan, *née* Smith, Kill and later of 54 Eccles Street, Dublin. Occupation: Grocer's Assistant. Residence: Dalkey, Dublin. Enlistment location: Kingstown. Died of wounds, France & Flanders, 8 August 1917. Age: 33. Memorial: XVII.D.12A, Lijssenthoek Military Cemetery.

S

SAVAGE, George: Rifleman, Royal Irish Rifles, 1st Battalion, 2967. Formerly RAMC. Son of Robert and Frances Savage, Donagh Patrick: Residence: Donagh Patrick: Educated: Wilson's Hospital, Multyfarnham. Brother of Robert, who was killed in the war. Their brother, Charles, survived the war but was severely wounded. Enlisted 1914 in the Royal Army Medical Corps in Dublin. Died: 4 March 1917. Age: 26. Memorial: Pier and Face 15A and 15B, Thiepval Memorial.

SAVAGE, Robert: Private. Royal Dublin Fusiliers, 1st Battalion, 25880. Born: Templemore. Son of Robert and Frances Savage, Donagh Patrick: Educated: Wilson's Hospital, Multyfarnham. Brother of George, who was killed in the war. Their brother, Charles, survived the war but was severely wounded. Killed in action, France & Flanders, 8 August 1918, first day of battle of Hindenberg line. Age: 31. Memorial: II.G.13, Borre British Cemetery.

SEERY, James: Guardsman, Scots Guards, 1st Battalion, 7636. Baptised: Oldcastle, 22 April 1888. Son of James and Mary Seery, née Gillick, Baltrasna, Moylough. Enlistment location: Liverpool. Served in France from 27 August 1914. Killed in action, France & Flanders, 11 November 1914. Memorial: Panel 11, Ypres (Menin Gate) Memorial.

SHEERIN, Joseph: Private, Royal Irish Fusiliers, 8th Battalion, 20131. Born: Yellow Furze. Residence: Beauparc. Enlistment location: Navan. Killed in action, France & Flanders, 7 July 1916. Memorial: Panel 124, Loos Memorial. From the *Meath Chronicle*, 5 August 1916, 'At the Navan Board of Guardians on Wednesday, on a motion of Mr. Kelly, seconded by Mr. Price, a vote of sympathy was passed with Mr. Collins (Master) brother in law and the relatives of the late Mr. James Sheerin, R.I.F. who was recently killed in the war.'

SHERIDAN, Bryan (Bernard): Corporal, 4th Canadian Mounted Rifles Battalion, 11 1452. Previously served two years with the Irish Guards. Born: Navan, 22 July 1885. Son of Thomas and Margaret Sheridan, née Kiernan, Trimgate Street, Navan and later of Grange Bective, Navan. Brother, William, also killed in the war. Another brother, Philip, was a prisoner of war but survived the war. Father's occupation: (1901) Shopkeeper, (1911) Farmer. Occupation: (1911) Clerk. Height: 5 foot 9 inches. Eyes: Blue. Hair: Brown. Enlisted 31 March 1915. Died: 3 June 1916. Memorial: Panel 30, 32, Ypres (Menin Gate) Memorial.

SHERIDAN, James John: Acting Company Quartermaster Sergeant, Lincolnshire Regiment, 1st Garrison Battalion, 19619. Formerly South Staffordshire Regiment, 10630. Born: Navan. Son of James and Sarah Sheridan. Husband of Sarah Sheridan, *née* Kelly, 74 Dumbarton Road, Clydebank, Glasgow. Enlistment location: Claybank, Dumbarton. Died: Malta, 28 January 1916. Age: 52. Memorial: C.VII.3, Pieta Military Cemetery.

SHERIDAN, Thomas: Private, Leinster Regiment, 7th Battalion, 5462. Born: Fordstown. Residence: Kells. Enlistment location: Drogheda. Died of wounds, France & Flanders, 1 February 1917. Memorial: I.F.23, Loker Churchyard.

SHERIDAN, Thomas: Private, Royal Irish Fusiliers, 8th Battalion, 16072. Born: Moynalty. Enlistment location: Drogheda. Died of wounds, France & Flanders, 23 March 1916. Memorial: I.H.129, Chocques Military Cemetery.

SHERIDAN, William: Private, Irish Guards, 1st Battalion, 5949. Baptised: Navan, 2 April 1894. Son of Thomas and Margaret Sheridan, *née* Kiernan, Trimgate Street, Navan and later of Grange Bective, Navan. Brother, Bryan, was also killed in the war. Another brother, Philip, was a prisoner of war but survived the war. Father's occupation: (1901) Shopkeeper, (1911) Farmer. Occupation: Farmer's son. Enlistment location: Navan. Served in France from 2 April 1915. Killed in action, France & Flanders, 18 May 1915. Age: 22. Memorial: Panel 4, Le Touret Memorial. From the *Meath Chronicle*, 3 July 1915:

Young Meathman Killed in the War

Deep regret has been occasioned in Bective district by the news that Mr. William Sheridan, seventh son of Mr. Thomas Sheridan and Mrs Sheridan, of Grange, Bective, has been killed at the front while fighting with the Irish Guards. Some months ago, the deceased, who was little more than twenty, joined the famous Irish regiment and after a brief training in England, was sent to the war. He was a young man of engaging disposition, cheerful, kindly and sport-loving, qualities which endeared him to many friends who have heard with heartfelt sorrow of his sad fate. It was characteristic of him that when the opportunity came he fearlessly faced the perils of a soldier's life, and now that he has fallen, when all the promises of life were before him, the thoughts of his youthful companions and all who knew him turn in fond and sad remembrance to the lonely grave where he sleeps in far-off France. With his bereaved father and mother and other members of the family, sincere and widespread sympathy is felt.

SHERLOCK, Peter: Private, Highland Light Infantry, 12th Service Battalion, 22376. Secondary Regiment: Royal Engineers, attached 253rd Company. Baptised: Donore, 17 September 1882. Son of Peter and Elizabeth Sherlock, *née* Daly, Donore and later of Rathgar, Dublin. Enlistment location: Wishaw, Lanarkshire. Served in France from 2 October 1915. Killed in action, France & Flanders, 1 September 1916. Age: 33. Memorial: VI.E.8, Vermelles British Cemetery.

SHERWOOD, John James: Private, Royal Inniskilling Fusiliers, 1st Battalion, 18326. Born: Oldcastle about 1896. Son of George and Elizabeth Sherwood, Glenboy, Oldcastle. Father's occupation: Labourer. Residence: Oldcastle. Enlistment location: Drogheda. Served in Balkans from 11 July 1915. Killed in action, France & Flanders, 1 July 1916. First day of the Battle of the Somme. Memorial: Pier and Face 4D and 5B, Thiepval Memorial.

SHERWOOD, William Eaton: Sapper, Royal Engineers, 205th Field Company, 121073. Born: Loughcrew. Son of James and Elizabeth Sherwood, Loughcrew, Oldcastle. Father's occupation: Stone Mason. Residence: Kells. Enlistment location: Drogheda.

Died of wounds, France & Flanders, 8 November 1918. Age: 26. Memorial: X.C.26, Terlincthun British Cemetery, Wimille. Sapper William Sherwood, R.E. (First World War Memorial, St Kieran's church, Loughcrew.)

SILLERY, Robert: Private, Labour Corps, 174653. Baptised: 31 August 1875. Son of Francis and Bridget Sillery, *née* Lynch, Clonbartan, Drumconrath. Father's occupation: Agricultural Labourer. Occupation: Agricultural Labourer. Died: 22 March 1919. Age: 40. Memorial: Drumconrath New Catholic Graveyard.

SKELLY, John: Bombardier, Royal Garrison Artillery, 258th Siege Battery, 25853. Born: Moynalty. Residence: Baltrasna, Moynalty. Enlistment location: Hamilton. Died of wounds, France & Flanders, 21 August 1917. Memorial: I.B.5, Godewaersvelde British Cemetery.

SOMERS, Patrick: Private, Royal Inniskilling Fusiliers, 1st Battalion, 32. Born: Derrygonnelly, Co. Tyrone. Son of James and Winifred Somers, Sligo. Husband of Catherine Somers, Old Cornmarket, Navan. Enlistment location: Enniskillen. Killled in action, Gallipoli, 21 August 1915. Age: 34. Memorial: Panel 97 to 101, Helles Memorial.

SMITH: Private, Fennor, Oldcastle. Died: September 1914. From the

Meath Chronicle, 3 October 1914, 'Oldcastle Men killed in the War. Deep regret has been occasioned in the Oldcastle district by the news that John Gaughran, Ballinlough; Private Smith, Fennor and Joseph Bergin, Oldcastle have been killed in the war.'

SMITH, Christopher: Private, Irish Guards, 2nd Battalion, 10782. Born: Burry, Kells about 1887. Son of Philip and Margaret Smith, Balgeeth. Father's occupation: Herd. Enlistment location: Navan. Killed in action, France & Flanders, 31 July 1917. Memorial: VI.B.12, Artillery Wood Cemetery. St Colmcille's Cemetery, Kells. From the *Meath Chronicle*, 18 August 1917, 'Private Christopher Smith, only son of Phillip Smith, of Ethelstown, has been reported killed at the Front on the 31st ult.'

SMITH, James: Private, Royal Dublin Fusiliers, 1st Battalion, 29329. Born: Culmullen about 1897. Son of Patrick and Margaret Smith, Bedfanstown, Crosskeys, Drumree. Father's occupation: Herd. Occupation: Telegraph Messenger. Residence: Drumree. Enlistment location: Dublin. Killed in action, France & Flanders, 5 October 1917. Age: 20. Memorial: Panel 144 to 145, Tyne Cot Memorial.

SMITH: *see* **CALLAN, Leo.**

SMITH, Patrick: Private, Irish Guards, 2nd Battalion, 10641. Baptised Moylough, Oldcastle, 7 October 1888. Son of John and Margaret Smith, *née* Gibney, Gortloney, Oldcastle. Father's occupation: Farmer. Occupation: Farmer's son. Enlistment location: Mullingar. Killed in action, France & Flanders, 23 March 1918. Memorial: Bay 1, Arras Memorial. Drogheda War Memorial.

SMITH, Patrick: Private, East Yorkshire Regiment, 2nd Battalion, 7161, Secondary Regiment: Labour Corps Secondary Unit transferred to (486815) 978th Company. Son of Dan and Ellen Smith, Dublin. Husband of Annie Smith, Cottage Row, Enfield. Died: Taranto, Italy, 5 October 1918. Age: 39. Memorial: III.H.7, Taranto Town Cemetery Extension, Italy.

SMYTH, Alexander: Private, Irish Guards, 2nd Battalion, 9351. Born: Athboy. Son of James and Mary Smyth, The Gardens, Killua, Clonmellon, Co. Westmeath. Residence: Mullingar. Enlistment location: Ballachulish, Argyle. Native of Dowestown, Cavan. Died of wounds, France & Flanders, 31 July 1917. Age: 21. Memorial: II.J.19, Dozinghem Military Cemetery.

SMYTH, Matthew: Private, Connaught Rangers, 1st Battalion, 8067. Baptised: Summerhill, 7 October 1883. Son of Thomas and Elizabeth Smyth, *née* Reilly, Clondoogan, Summerhill. Father's occupation: Agricultural Labourer. Occupation:

Agricultural Labourer. Residence: Summerhill. Enlistment location: Dublin. Served in France from 14 August 1914. Killed in action, France & Flanders, 19 March 1915. Memorial: Panel 43, Le Touret Memorial.

SMYTH, Nicholas: Lance-Corporal, Royal Dublin Fusiliers, 1st Battalion, 10935. Baptised: Duleek, 13 November 1887. Son of Edward and Brigid Smyth, née Mitchell, Bolies, Duleek and later of Loughlinstown, Tara. Father's occupation: Farm Servant. Residence: Duleek. Enlistment location: Dublin. Served in Balkans from 25 April 1915. Killed in action, Gallipoli, 30 April 1915. Age: 27. Memorial: Special Memorial B. 101, V Beach Cemetery.

SMYTH, Patrick: Private, Leinster Regiment, 2nd Battalion, 5250. Born: Drumconrath. Enlistment location: Drumconrath. Killed in action, France & Flanders, 27 March 1918. Memorial: Panel 78, Pozieres Memorial.

SMYTH, Philip: Private, Connaught, Rangers, 2nd Battalion, 10639. Baptised: Kells, 23 August 1896. Son of Michael and Mary Smith, née McNamee, Cannon Street, Kells and later of Norbinstown, Carterstown, Kells. Father's occupation: Labourer. Residence: Kells. Enlistment location: Drogheda. Taken as a prisoner of war in August 1914 during the retreat from Mons. Died of pneumonia in a German Prisoner of War Camp, 11 August 1918. Age: 21. Memorial: V.L.8, Niederzwehren Cemetery.

SMYTH, Thomas: Private, Royal Irish Fusiliers, 2nd Battalion, C Company, 9816. Formerly East Lancashire Regiment, 9503. Baptised: Navan, 9 September 1887. Son of Peter and Rosanna Smyth, née Boland, Chapel Lane, Navan. Father's occupation: Shoemaker. Enlistment location: Dublin. Served in France from 19 December 1914. Killed in action, France & Flanders, 25 May 1915. Age: 27. Memorial: Panel 42, Ypres (Menin Gate) Memorial.

SMYTH, William: Private, Leinster Regiment, 2nd Battalion, 5408. Baptised: Trim, 16 August 1898. Son of Patrick and Anne Smyth, née Gallagher, Dalystown, later of Clonee, Ballivor and later of Donore, Hill of Down. Father's occupation: Farm Labourer. Enlistment location: Trim. Killed in action, France & Flanders, 30 May 1918. Age: 20. Memorial: F.11, Cinq Rues British Cemetery, Hazebrouk. His cousin, James McManus, Dalystown, Trim, was also killed in the war.

SODEN, Christopher: Private, Royal Dublin Fusiliers, 2nd Battalion, 8581. Baptised: Kells, 15 December 1874. Son of Thomas and Anne Soden, née Brown. Husband of Mary Soden, 29 Upper Kevin Street, Dublin.

Occupation: General Labourer. Enlistment location: Dublin. Served in France from 1 April 1915. Killed in action, France & Flanders, 24 May 1915. Age: 39. Memorial: Panel 44 and 46, Ypres (Menin Gate) Memorial.

SOUTHWELL, Thomas: Private, Royal Dublin Fusiliers, 10th Battalion, 26027. Born: Barristown. Son of Michael Southwell, Barristown, Slane. Residence: Stackallen. Enlistment location: Liverpool. Died, at home, 18 April 1916. Age: 28. Memorial: Hill of Slane Cemetery.

STACPOOLE: *see* **DE STACPOOLE**

STEWART, John: Corporal, Cheshire Regiment, 10th Battalion, W/891. Born: Co. Monaghan or Co. Cavan. Son of John and Hannah Stewart, *née* Kelvey, Donore, Moynalty and later of Westland, Moynalty, Kells. Father's occupation: (1901) Agricultural Labourer, (1911) Coachman. Occupation: Domestic Servant. Residence: Kells. Enlistment location: Port Sunlight, Cheshire. Served in France from 25 September 1915. Wounded late 1915 and on recovery returned to France. Killed in action, France & Flanders, 6 June 1918. Age: 24. Memorial: II.B.9, Jonchery-sur-Vesle British Cemetery.

STONES, Patrick: Private, Lancashire Fusiliers, 9th Battalion, 27914. Formerly King's Own Yorkshire Light Infantry, 23676. Born: Trim. Son of James and Mary Stones, Corporationland, Trim. Father's occupation: Farmer. Residence: Clonbun. Occupation: Farmer's son. Enlistment location: Dewsbury, Yorkshire. Killed in action, France & Flanders, 4 October 1917. Age: 32. Memorial: Panel 54 to 60 and 163A, Tyne Cot Memorial.

STONE, Jos: Gnr RFA (Trim Church of Ireland, Roll of Honour) A Joseph Stones did serve with the Royal Field Artillery but is not listed as being killed in the war. Patrick had a younger brother, Joseph.

STRAIN, Alex: Private, Royal Inniskilling Fusiliers, 1st Battalion, 20860. Born: Rathmullan, Co. Meath. Son of Alex and Julia Brogan Strain and husband of Brigid Diver Strain. Enlistment location: Clydebank. Served in Balkans from 18 July 1915. Died of wounds, Gallipoli, 28 August 1915. Age: 44. Memorial: F.187, Alexandria (Chatby) Military and War Memorial Cemetery, Egypt. Drogheda War Memorial.

T

TEELING, Thomas: Private, Leinster Regiment, 2nd Battalion, 5739. Born: Finchley, Middlesex, 20 July 1879. Married to Mary and at least one child, Mary Christina. Residence: Kells. Enlistment location: Navan. Occupation: Farm Labourer. Served in France from 8 September 1914. Killed in action, France & Flanders, 11 April 1915. Memorial: B.15, Ferme Buterne Military Cemetery, Houplines. From the *Meath Chronicle*, 24 April 1915:

Meath Soldier Killed in Action
News reached Kells during the week that Private Thomas Teeling, a native of Headfort had been killed in action in the fight at Neuve Chapelle. Poor Teeling, who was a reservist, had been working for some years with Mrs Rothwell, Rockfield.

THUNDER, Michael Hubert Francis: Second Lieutenant, Royal Flying Corps. Born: 5 September 1879, Ramsgate. Son of George and Margaret Thunder, *née* Pugin, Lagore, Ratoath. Father's occupation: Major. Occupation: Mining Engineer. Received Royal Aero Club Aviators' Certificate on Maurice Farman Biplane, at the Military School, Ruislip, on 16 January 1916. Died of burns, Norwich Hospital, 24 September 1916. Memorial: Ramsgate (St Augustine) Roman Catholic Churchyard. From *Flight*:

Second Lieutenant Michael H.F. Thunder of the RFC who died at Norwich from burns received in a flying accident, who was buried at Ramsgate on September 29th (1916) with military honours. He was son of the late George Thunder, of Lagore, Meath and grandson on his mother's side of Pugin, the architect. He was educated at St Augustine's College, Ramsgate; he had his commission in December 1915, and was gazateered flying officer in March of this year. Six officers of the Flying Corps acted as bearers and the officer in command arrived by aeroplane.

From the *Meath Chronicle*, 7 October 1916, 'Second-Lieut. Michael H.F. Thunder of the Royal Flying Corps, youngest son of the late George Thunder, Lagore, died 24th ult at Norwich Hospital from burns resulting from a flying accident.'

TINLEY, John: Royal Irish Fusiliers, 2nd Battalion, 20437. Born: Dunshaughlin. Residence: Bailieborough, Co. Cavan. Enlistment location: Cavan. Died: Egypt, 30

December 1917. Memorial: Chatby Memorial.

TISDALL, Charles Arthur: Major, Irish Guards, 1st Battalion. Eldest son of Captain John Knox Tisdall and husband of Gwynneth May R. Tisdall. Born in 1875. Killed in action near Villiers Cotterets, France & Flanders, 1 September 1914. Age: 39. Memorial: II.2, Guards' Grave, Villiers Cotterets Forest. As a young man he joined the Irish Guards. He inherited the Tisdall estate in 1895 when he was 20 years old, a total of 3,962 acres in Meath, 493 in Limerick and 5,775 in Kilkenny. He leased out the estate. Major Tisdall was killed just a month after the war broke out, killed in action in the retreat from Mons in Belgium. From War Memorial, 1914-1918, Kells Church of Ireland, 'Captain C.A. Tisdall, Irish Guards.' From Julianstown church stained-glass window, 'Charles Arthur Tisdall, Captain Irish Guards, killed in action at Villiers Cottereto 1st September 1914.' From the *Meath Chronicle*, 28 November 1914:

Meathmen Killed and Wounded Captain C. A. Tisdall, Irish Guards, is now reported killed at Villiers Catterets. He was the eldest son of the late Captain J.K. Tisdall, R.E. and succeeded his grandfather, Mr. John Tisdall, J.P. D.L. Charlesfort, Meath in 1892. He joined the Irish Rifles in 1900, and was the next year transferred to the Guards.

A relative of his, Sub-Lieutenant A.W. St Clair Tisdall, won the VC for distinguished gallantry at Gallipoli, in rescuing under heavy fire, several wounded men on the beach during the landing from the River Clyde on 25 April 1915. Another relative Lieutenant C.D. Tisdall M.C. Irish Guards was killed 15 September 1916.

TUITE, James: Private, Australian Infantry, AIF, 36th Battalion, 3146. Baptised: Oldcastle, 21 January 1883. Son of James and Elizabeth Tuite, *née* Kelaghan, Oldcastle. Father's occupation: Grocer, Farmer and JP. Occupation: (1901) Apprentice, (1916) Farmhand. Height: 5 foot 8 inches. Eyes: Blue. Hair: Light Brown. Enlisted: 6 October 1916. Killed in action, France & Flanders, 6 April 1918. Age: 35. Memorial: Villers-Bretonneux Memorial. Memorial: St Brigid's Graveyard, Oldcastle. From the *Meath Chronicle*, 22 September 1917:

As a result of the recent "big push" on the western front, many Oldcastle names occur in the casualty lists, including Mr. Webb, Hilltown, Mr. Berry, Loughcrew, also a man named Tuite, who belonged to the Australian contingent.

TULLY, John: Rifleman, Royal Irish Rifles, 2nd Battalion, B Company,

19998. Born: Kells. Son of Luke and Kate Tully, Fair Green, Navan. Enlistment location: Navan. Served in the Balkans from 22 July 1915. Killed in action, France & Flanders, 19 May 1916. Age: 30. Memorial: Bay 9, Arras Memorial. From the *Meath Chronicle*, 3 June 1916, 'News has reached Navan of the death of John Tully, Fair Green, who belonged to the Irish Guards. He was killed in action at the front.'

TYNAN, William: Lance-Corporal, Leinster Regiment, 2nd Battalion, 4231. Born: Killashee, Co. Longford. Son of Joseph H. Tynan, MD and Anne, *née* Carroll, of Oldcastle. Husband of Mary Tynan, *née* Moore, 14 Auburn Avenue, Dublin. Residence: Dublin. Enlistment location: Portstmouth. Killed in action, France & Flanders, 12 April 1917. Age: 31. Memorial: Lievin Communal Cemetery Extension.

V

VANCROFT, Evan: Private, Irish Guards, 1st Battalion, 2335. Born: Navan. Enlistment location: Dublin. Served in France from 13 August 1914. Killed in action, 3 November 1914. Memorial: II.B.20, Ypres Town Cemetery Extension.

VAUGHEY, John: Private, Leinster Regiment, 2nd Battalion, 5143. Born: Slane. Enlistment location: Navan. Killed in action, France & Flanders, 27 March 1918. Memorial: Panel 78, Pozieres Memorial. Drogheda War Memorial.

W

WADE, George Edward: Lance-Corporal, Essex Regiment, 2nd Battalion, 8029. Born: Bromley-by-Bow, Middlesex. Son of Henry and Jane Wade, 104 Fairfoot Road, Bow, London. Husband of Josephine Wade, later Mangan, Grennanstown, Stamullin. Residence: Dublin. Enlistment location: Warley, Essex. Killed in action, France & Flanders, 8 May 1915. Age: 30. Memorial: Panel 139., Ypres (Menin Gate) Memorial.

WALLACE: Private. Irish Guards. Native of Kilkenny. Mother resided at St Patrick's Rectory, Trim. (Horneck)

WALL, Christopher Joseph: Corporal, Royal Dublin Fusiliers, 1st Battalion, 24478. Baptised: Dunboyne, 4 May 1892. Son of Patrick and Alice Walls, née Begley, Jarretstown. Father's occupation: Groom. Enlistment location: London. Killed in action, France & Flanders, 20 November 1917. Awards: DCM. Memorial: II.C.19, Croisilles British Cemetery.

WALL, John: Private, Irish Guards, 2nd Battalion, 6396. Born: Duleek. Enlistment location: Drogheda. Killed in action, France & Flanders, 27 September 1916. Memorial: III.W.5, Guards' Cemetery, Lesboeufs. Drogheda War Memorial.

WALL, Patrick: Lance-Corporal, Leinster Regiment, 2nd Battalion, 5469. Born: Ardcath. Son of Thomas and Annie Wall, Hawkinstown, Piercetown, Rathfeigh. Father's occupation: Herd. Occupation: Shepherd. Killed in action, France & Flanders, 27 March 1918. Age: 27. Memorial: Panel 78, Pozieres Memorial.

WALL, Patrick: Private, Royal Irish Regiment, 2nd Battalion, 18420. Formerly Royal Dublin Fusiliers, 30552. Baptised: Dunboyne, 11 March 1888. Son of Patrick and Alice Walls, née Begley, Jarretstown. Father's occupation: Groom. Residence: Dunboyne. Enlistment location: Dublin. Died of wounds, France & Flanders, 6 June 1918. Memorial: II.D.6, Ebblinghem Military Cemetery.

WALSH, Charles Joseph: Irish Guards. Baptised: Navan, 5 May 1886. Son of Joseph and Rose Walsh, née Bird, Watergate Street. Father's occupation: Watchmaker/Jeweller. Occupation: Watchmaker/Jeweller. Served in Navan Irish National Volunteers. Seriously wounded at Neuve Chapelle, 18 May 1915. Died from wounds, Navan, 26 November 1919. Memorial: New Cemetery, Boyne Road, Navan. From the *Meath Chronicle*, 29 November 1919:

With much regret we record the death of Mr. Charles J. Walsh, which took place on Wednesday night after a lingering illness at Navan. Deceased, who was a fine type of young Irish manhood, standing over six feet high, was a member of the old National Volunteers, and at the outbreak of war he responded to the call made by the late Mr. John E. Redmond, and joined the Irish Guards. After the usual period of training he was sent to France, where he saw much service for several months. Conveying a despatch in the front line of trenches, a German shell exploded in his vicinity, and he was blown into the air, and coming to earth was buried in a pile of debris. Severe injury to the spine was the result, and having spent eighteen weary months in hospital in England, he returned home practically a physical wreck. Before joining the army the late Mr. Walsh assisted his brother, Mr Alfred Walsh, in the watch-making and jewellery business carried on in Navan, and was well and favourably known to a wide circle. A lover of outdoor sports, Charlie, as he was popularly known, was the best of good fellows, a true friend, genial companion, one of those whom to know was to love and esteem. After his sorrowing young widow and two little children and other immediate relatives, his old school-fellows and companions will most poignantly feel his premature demise – he was little more than 30 years of age. A member of one of the oldest and most respected families in the town, his sad fate is genuinely lamented by rich and poor, and the expressions of sincere condolence to those so tragically bereaved are many. R.I.P.

WALSH, Edward: Private, Irish Guards, 1st Battalion, 3409. Baptised: Stamullin, 14 January 1889. Son of Patrick and Anne Walsh, *née* Kennedy, Herbertstown. Father's occupation: Shepherd. Enlistment location: Drogheda. Served in France from 21 September 1914. Killed in action, France & Flanders, 18 November 1914. Memorial: Panel II, Ypres (Menin Gate) Memorial. Drogheda War Memorial.

WALSH, Michael: Private, Loyal North Lancashire Regiment, 1st Battalion, 16784. Baptised: Summerhill, 20 April 1879. Son of Michael and Christina Walsh, *née* Feeney, Summerhill. Mother's occupation: Lodging Housekeeper. Occupation: Labourer. Enlistment location: Bolton. Served in France from 30 September 1915. Killed accidentally, France & Flanders, 9 January 1916. Memorial: III.K.15, Dud Corner Cemetery, Loos.

WALSH, Patrick: Private, Leinster Regiment, 7th Battalion, 5183. Born:

Duleek. Son of Thomas and Margaret Walsh, Painestown. Husband of Catherine Walsh, Dean Hill, Hayes, Navan. Two children: Thomas and Catherine. Residence: Navan. Enlistment location: Navan. Killed in action, France & Flanders, 9 March 1917. Memorial: K.7, Pond Farm Cemetery.

WALTON, Albert: Private, Machine Gun Corps (Infantry), 1st Battalion, 112th Company, 8894. Formerly Northumberland Fusiliers, 23514. Born: Navan. Son of Mr and Mrs F.G. Walton. Enlistment location: Canterbury. Killed in action, France & Flanders, 10 July 1916. Age: 34. Memorial: 4.G.33, London Cemetery and Extension, Longueval.

WARD, Patrick: Staff-Sergeant, Cheshire Regiment, 2nd Battalion, 7180. Warrant Officer, sub-conductor of Supply and Transport, promoted to officer's commission on death-bed, Indian Army. Born: Jordanstown, Enfield. Residence: Clara, Co. Offaly. Enlistment location: Birkenhead, Cheshire. Served in Africa from 10 November 1914. Died from Blackwater fever, Sindi, German East Africa, 28 December 1917. Age: 23. Awards: MSM. Mentioned in dispatches. Memorial: 6.A.10, Dar es Salaam War Cemetery.

WARD, Simon: Private, Irish Guards, 2nd Battalion, 9732. Baptised:

Navan, June 1880. Son of Mary Ward. Mother's occupation: Seamstress. Husband of Elizabeth Ward, 71 St Paul Street, Dublin. Occupation: (1901) Stable Boy. Enlistment location: Dublin. Killed in action, France & Flanders, 9 October 1917. Age: 36. Memorial: Panel 10 to 11, Tyne Cot Memorial.

WATSON, John: Private, Royal Dublin Fusiliers, 10th Battalion, 16294. Born: Kilcock, Co. Kildare. Son of Anne Watson, Connaught Street, Kilcock, Co. Kildare. Enlistment location: Naas. Served in France from 20 December 1915. Wounded, 1916. Died: France & Flanders, 30 October 1918. Age: 23. Memorial: Balfeaghan Graveyard. Balfeaghan Graveyard – '16294 Private J. Watson, Royal Dublin Fusiliers 30th October 1918 aged 23'.

WATSON, Thomas: Gunner, Royal Field Artillery, 50th Battery, 34th Brigade, 116062. Born: Oldcastle. Died of wounds, France & Flanders, 19 October 1917. Memorial: P.III.M.10B, St Sever Cemetery Extension, Rouen.

WEBB: From the *Meath Chronicle*, 22 September 1917, 'As a result of the recent "big push" on the Western Front, many Oldcastle names occur in the casualty lists, including Mr. Webb, Hilltown, Mr. Berry, Loughcrew, also a man named Tuite, who belonged to the Australian contingent.'

WHELEHAN, James: Private, Drummer, Leinster Regiment, 7th Battalion, 9295. Baptised: Navan, 6 October 1890. Son of Peter and Julia Whelehan, *née* Doogan, Cannon Row, Navan. Father's occupation: Cloth Finisher. Enlistment location: Navan. Served in France from 22 February 1915. Died of wounds, France & Flanders, 12 June 1917. Memorial: III,C.62, Bailleul Communal Cemetery Extension (Nord).

WHITE, Joseph: Private, Irish Guards, 2nd Battalion, 8843. Born: Heronstown. Son of Joseph and Bridget White, Killary. Husband of Mary White, Killary, Lobinstown. Enlistment location: Drogheda. Died of wounds, France & Flanders, 15 April 1918. Age: 31. Memorial: Div.62. III.D.4, Ste. Marie Cemetery, Le Havre. Drogheda War Memorial.

WHYTE, Bernard: Private, Machine Gun Corps (Infantry), 1st Battalion, 11th Company, 6112. Formerly Leinster Regiment, 10554. Born: Dunshaughlin. Enlistment location: Navan. Died of wounds, France & Flanders, 27 July 1916. Memorial: E. 7340, Cheltenham Cemetery.

WHYTE, John: Corporal, Royal Dublin Fusiliers, 6th Battalion, 11432. Baptised: Skryne, 29 June 1893. Son of Thomas and Elizabeth Whyte, *née* Murtagh, Painestown, Dunshaughlin. Father's occupation: Agricultural Labourer. Residence: Dunshaughlin. Enlistment location: Drogheda. Served in France from 23 August 1914. Killed in action, France & Flanders, 8 October 1918. Memorial: C.3, Beaurevoir British Cemetery.

WILLIAMSON, Jack: Private, Army Veterinary Corps, SE/33399. Born: Co. Armagh. Son of William and Sarah Williamson, Black Castle, Navan. Father's occupation: Coachman. Occupation: General Labourer. Enlistment location: Ironbridge. Drowned at sea, RMS *Leinster* 10 October 1918. Age: 24. Memorial: Hollybrook Memorial, Southampton.

WYLLIE, James: Private, Cameronians, Scottish Rifles, 2nd Battalion, A/7692. Born: Trim. Son of Jane Wiley, Sarsfield Avenue, Trim. Mother's occupation: Labourer and Servant. Occupation: General Labourer. Enlistment location: Hamilton. Served in France from 17 February 1915. Died of wounds, France & Flanders, 11 February 1916. Memorial: VI.C.17A, Etaples Military Cemetery.

Y

YORE, Peter: Private, Australian Infantry, AIF, 11th Battalion, 6843. Baptised: Carnaross, 3 March 1884. Son of George and Elizabeth Yore, *née* Farrelly, Rahendrick. Father's occupation: Farmer. Occupation: (1901) Farmer's son, (1916) Railway Employee. Emigrated to Blackpool in 1907 and worked as a gardener/farm hand at a convent. Emigrated to Australia in 1909 working his way on the ship, *Omrah*. Wife: Bridget Mary (Delia) Yore, *née* Reilly. They met in Blackpool and married in Fremantle in 1912. Daughter: Mary Elizabeth. Residence: 2 Letitia Road, North Fremantle, Western Australia. Enlisted: 12 June 1916. Enlistment location: Albany, Western Australia. Height: 5 foot 6 inches. Eyes: Grey. Hair: Dark. Embarked at Freemantle on HMAT *Argyleshire*, 9 November 1916. In King George Hospital from 27 January 1917 to 12 February 1917. Served in France from 15 May 1917. Killed in action, France & Flanders, 20 September 1917. Memorial: Panel 7-17-23-25-27-29-31, Ypres (Menin Gate) Memorial.

Casualties Broken Down by Area

Not a complete list

Athboy

BAYLY, Maurice Fitzgerald.
CERUMNEY, James.
COLEMAN, Thomas.
CONLON, Richard.
CONNOLLY, Patrick.
CUNNIFFE, John.
GAFFNEY, Richard.
GLYNN, John.
GREY, George Rochfort.
LYNCH, Patrick.
McCLOREY, Owen.
McGUIRES, S.
MURPHY, Denis.
PALMER, Arthur.
REILLY, Patrick.
SMYTH, Alexander.

Ballivor

BLIGH, John.
BLIGH, Thomas.
CONLON, Owen.
GANNON, William.
MAHON, Matthew J.

Donore

BYRNE, George.
CAMPBELL, James.
COOGAN, Michael.
COYLE, Patrick.
FINEGAN, William.
LEONARD, John.
McDONNELL, Patrick.
SHERLOCK, Peter.

Drogheda

AHEARNE, Michael James,
  Bettystown.
BRENNAN, James John, Julianstown.
BRODIGAN, Francis John, Pilltown.
CAIRNES, William, Jameson.
CODDINGTON, Hubert John,
  Oldbridge.
DEMPSEY, Patrick, St Mary's.
HEALY, William, St Mary's.
HENRY, Michael, Colpe.
KENEALLY, Charles, Laytown.
KENNY, Thomas, Born SLANE.
KING, Lawrence.
MCCANN, Joseph, Colpe West.
McCONNON, Matthew J.
McDONALD, Alexander, Laytown.
McDONNELL, John, Kilsharvan.
McEVOY, Patrick, Donacarney.
McEVOY, Thomas, Donacarney.
McGRANE, Peter, Julianstown.
McGRANE, William, Julianstown.
MURTAGH, William, St Mary's.
OSBORNE, Geoffrey William,
  Julianstown.
REYNOLDS, Frederick,
  Mornington.

Drumconrath

CALLAN, Leo.
CAROLAN, Terence.
CASSIDY, Richard.
CULLITON, Edward.
CURTIS, Bernard.
DUNNE, Hugh.
KEELAN, Joseph, Meath Hill.
McEVOY, Richard, Heronstown.
REILLY, William, Lobinstown.
SILLERY, Robert.
SMYTH, Patrick.
WHITE, Joseph.

Duleek

BRIEN, John.
CLARKE, Cornelius.
CONLON, Thomas.
GAVIN, James.
GIBNEY, John.
GOGARTY, Matthew.
GORMAN, James.
GRADWELL, George Francis. Platten.
HAMMICK, St Vincent Charles Farrant.
HATCH, Nicholas Stephen.
HEENEY, Samuel.
HOEY, James.
O'KEEFFE, Joseph Richard.
LANGAN, Eugene.
LANGAN, James.
McKEON, John.
POTTER, John.
SMYTH, Nicholas.
WALL, John.

WALL, Patrick.
WALSH, Patrick.

Dunboyne

CRONE, David.
DUNNE, Patrick.
GAISFORD, Robert Sandeman.
GANNON, James.
LEONARD, Patrick.
McLOUGHLIN, Thomas.
MALONE, Patrick.
MEEHAN, Peter.
MOONEY, James, Clonee.
MULLEN, James, Roddinstown.
MULLEN, Patrick Joseph, Roddinstown.
O'NEILL, Patrick.
WALL, Christopher Joseph.
WALL, Patrick.

Dunshaughlin

ALLEN, Patrick Christopher.
DEASE, Maurice James, Culmullin.
DORAN, John.
DOREY, John.
FOLEY, Christopher.
LONERGAN, Daniel, Culmullin.
LONERGAN, John Francis, Culmullin.
RAFFERTY, Patrick.
ROGERS, James, Drumree.
SMITH, James, Drumree.
TINLEY, John.
WHYTE, Bernard.

Enfield

COLGAN, John.
CRYAN, Patrick.
FARRINGTON, John Joseph.
FOWLER, George Glynn.
FURLONG, Patrick.
HILL, Edward.
HILL, Patrick.
MULALLEY, John.
MURPHY, Christopher.
REILLY, John.
ROURKE, John, Rathcore.
RYAN, Hugh Joseph, Kill.
SMITH, Patrick.
WARD, Patrick.

Kells and district

AUGHEY, John.
AUGHEY, Owen.
BARNES, Peter Joseph, Carnaross.
BARNEWALL, The Hon. Reginald
  Nicholas Francis Mary.
BENNETT, James.
BOND, Alfred.
BRADY, Edward.
BRADY, Francis.
CARROLL, Frederick Stanley.
COYLE, Michael.
DEVINE, Patrick.
DRUM, Michael.
FARRELL, Patrick.
GEOGHEGAN, Michael.
GERAGHTY, Patrick.
GRIFFIN, James.
HEALY, Guy Bambant.
HIGGINS, Patrick.

HOLMES, Oliver Wendall.
HOPKINS, James.
IRVINE, William, Allenstown.
IRWIN, Thomas.
JENKIN, Victor David.
LEDDY, Patrick. Served as DOLAN.
LEDDY, Peter.
LYNCH, Patrick, Carnaross.
McCABE, Andrew.
McCORMICK, John Hugh
  Gardiner.
McCORMACK, Thomas.
McDERMOTT, Matthew.
McDONNELL, James.
McENROE, Herbert Joseph.
McMAHON, Joseph.
McPARTLAND, John.
McPARTLAND, Matthew.
McWHIRTER, Robert.
MAGUIRE, George.
MAGUIRE, Patrick.
MARKEY, John, Carlanstown/Kilbeg.
MARKEY, Thomas, Carlanstown/
  Kilbeg.
MASTERSON, Michael.
MOLLOY, Thomas.
MULVANEY, James.
MULVANEY, Thomas.
MURPHY, John.
MURRAY, William Frederick.
PIGOTT, William Gregory.
RADCLIFFE, Herbert Gravers.
REILLY, John.
REILLY, Thomas.
RUSSELL, Andrew Joseph.
SAVAGE, George.
SAVAGE, Robert.
SHERIDAN, Thomas, Fordstown.
SMITH, Christopher.

SMYTH, Philip.
SODEN, Christopher.
TEELING, Thomas.
TISDALL, Charles Arthur,
  Charlesfort.
TULLY, John.
YORE, Peter, Carnaross.

LANCASTER, Thomas Arthur
  Victor.
MATTOCK, Robert Clement, Hill
  of Down.
MATTOCK, Thomas Southwood,
  Hill of Down.
WATSON, John, Kilcock.

Kentstown

BOHAN, Robert Joseph.
BOHAN, William.
CRINION, Michael.
DALY, John, Monkstown.
FAY, Michael, Kenstown.

Kilmessan/Dunsany

DOHERTY, Thomas, Dunsany.
HANLEY, Owen.
LYNCH, John.
MADDEN, Patrick Joseph.
PRESTON, Arthur John Dillon.

Kilmore

CONNOR, Christopher.

Kinnegad and southwest Meath

COLLINS, James.
DARBY, John.
LANCASTER, Charles Edward
  Archibald, Ballyboggan.

Longwood

DE STACPOOLE, Robert Andrew
DE STACPOOLE, Roderick
  Algernon Anthony.
DIXON, Michael.
EBBITT, Joseph.
FLYNN, Patrick.
HUSSEY, Patrick.
KILLEEN, Michael.

Moynalty

DALY, James.
MAGAN, Frederick.
MARSHALL-BARNES, Alfred
  Hubert.
MUNROE, Patrick.
O'BRIEN, Christopher Owen.
O'BRIEN, Owen.
REILLY, James.
REILLY, Michael.
SHERIDAN, Thomas.
SKELLY, John.
STEWART, John.

Navan and district

BLAKE, John.
BOYLAN, Joseph.
BRADY, John, Dunderry.
BRENNAN, Patrick.
BRIEN, William Thomas,
 Randalstown.
CAHILL, James.
CALLAGHAN, John, Castletown.
CARROLL, J.
CARROLL, Matthew.
CASEY, Christopher.
CASSERLY, Edward, Bohermeen.
CASSIDY, Edward, Bohermeen.
CASSIDY, Joseph.
CASSIDY, Thomas, Harristown.
CLARKIN, Patrick, Robinstown.
CLINTON, Thomas.
COLCLOUGH, Michael Joseph.
COLLINS, George.
COWLEY, Joseph.
CREGAN, Patrick Joseph.
DARBY, Patrick, Johnstown.
DODDS, William.
DONNELLY, Thomas.
DONOHOE, Joseph.
DOUGHERTY, Thomas.
DUIGNAN, Bernard.
FAY, James. Johnstown.
FITZPATRICK, Edward, Johnstown.
FITZSIMONS, Frank.
FLANAGAN, James.
FOX, Patrick.
GALLIGAN, Patrick.
GALLIGAN, Thomas.
GERRARD, Christopher,
 Bohermeen.
GILBERT, James.

GILES, Victor Marshall.
GORMAN, Joseph.
HAMILTON, Lawrence.
HARLIN, Arthur Joseph.
HAROLD, Thomas Francis.
HEARY, Thomas.
HENNESSY, Patrick Andrew.
HODGINS, Joseph Thomas,
 Faughanhill.
HOLDEN, Sidney Naldrett.
JENKINS, William, Ardbraccan.
KANE, Patrick.
KEALY, William.
KEAPPOCK, John.
KERRIGAN, Joseph.
LEGGE-BOURKE, Nigel Walter
 Henry, Hayes.
LEONARD, Michael Joseph.
LOWRY, Joseph Ewart, Bachelor's
 Lodge.
LYONS, Christopher, Ardbraccan.
McDONNELL, Patrick.
McLOUGHLIN, James,
 Tankardstown.
MASTERSON, Michael.
MASTERSON, Patrick.
MASTERSON, Patrick.
MATHIESON, Kenneth Ronald,
 Tara.
MATTHEWS, John.
METGE, Rudolph C. Athlumney.
MONAGHAN, Lawrence.
MONAGHAN, Thomas.
MOORE, Patrick.
MULDOON, Philip.
MULVANEY, Joseph.
MURPHY, Joseph.
MURPHY, Peter.
NEVINS, Eugene.

O'BRIEN, Joseph.
O'KEEFFE, Christopher.
O'NEILL, Christopher.
O'ROURKE, Christopher.
OWENS, William, Hayes.
PETTIGRUE, Thomas Percy, Ardbraccan.
PHILLIPS, John Paul, Wilkinstown.
PHILLIPS, Michael.
PIERCE, Thomas.
QUINN, James.
REILLY, James.
REILLY, John.
REILLY, John, Randlestown.
REILLY, Patrick.
REILLY, Patrick.
REILLY, William, Ardbraccan.
RENNICKS, Richard, Ardbraccan.
ROGERS, Christopher.
SHEERIN, Joseph.
SHERIDAN, Bryan.
SHERIDAN, James John.
SHERIDAN, William.
SOMERS, Patrick.
SMYTH, Thomas.
VANCROFT, Evan.
WALSH, Charles.
WALTON, Albert.
WARD, Simon.
WHELEHAN, James.
WILLIAMSON, Jack.

Nobber

BLIGH, Frederick Arthur.
ENGLISHBY, James.
HAGERTY, John.
McCANN, Cornelius.

O'REILLY, Hugh, Kilmainhamwood
O'REILLY, William, Kilmainhamwood.

Oldcastle

ARMSTRONG, John.
ARMSTRONG, William.
BERRY, Harry Albert, Loughcrew.
CASSIDY, James Joseph, Ross.
DOWNEY, Eugene.
DRUMGOOLE, John.
FARRELL, James.
GAFFNEY, John, Ross.
GAUGHRAN, Thomas, Ballinlough.
GIBNEY, James.
GIBSON, Walter David.
GLANCY, James, Ballinlough.
KELLETT, Thomas, Seymourstown.
KIERNAN, James Leo.
KIERNAN, Patrick.
LOWNDES, Thomas.
McENROE, James, Ballinlough.
McGUIRE, Joseph.
McLARNEY, John.
McPHILLIPS, Joseph.
MAHON, Hugh.
MARLOW, Charles Dwyer.
MOSS, David, Loughcrew.
NAPER, Francis C., Loughcrew.
NAPER, George Wyatt Edgell, Loughcrew.
O'NEILL, Thomas, Loughcrew.
SEERY, James.
SHERWOOD, John James.
SHERWOOD, William Eaton.
SMITH, Patrick.

TUITE, James.
TYNAN, William.
WATSON, Thomas.

Oristown

CALLAGHAN, Michael.
HORAN, William.
KENNEDY, Thomas.
MINCH, John.
MURRAY, Patrick.

Ratoath/Ashbourne

BRADY, James.
CARR, John, Ashbourne.
CLARKE, Michael Joseph.
CLARKE, Joseph.
DONNELLY, John.
DUNNE, John Joseph, Curraha.
FORTUNE, Christopher.
MITCHELL, Christopher, Curraha.
MITCHELL, John, Curraha.
O'TOOLE, James.
PLUNKETT, Hugh, Crickstown.
THUNDER, Michael Hubert
  Francis, Lagore.

Skryne

CONNOR, Patrick.
DUFFY, Bernard.
HUGHES, Bernard.
MURDOCK, Charles Walter,
  Rathfeigh.

WALL, Patrick, Rathfeigh.
WHYTE, John.

Slane and district

BRUTON, Charles, Beauparc.
CAMPBELL, Hugh, Beauparc.
CAREY, Edward, Rathkenny.
CAROLAN, Laurence.
CLARKE, real name LANE, served
  as Clarke, James.
CONYNGHAM, Victor George
  Henry Francis.
CRONIN, Gerald George.
FARRELL, Francis.
FEELEY, William, Stackallen.
FITZPATRICK, Patrick.
FLOOD, Michael Joseph.
FLOOD, Patrick.
GRIFFIN, Thomas, Fennor.
HALPIN, Edward, Killary.
HALPIN, John, Killary.
HALPIN, Matthew, Barristown.
LANE, Charles Willington Tremayne,
  Rathkenny.
LEDWIDGE, Francis Edward.
LYNAGH, Patrick.
LYNCH, Charles Joseph.
McCONNON, James.
McCONNON, William.
McGRATH, Richard.
MURPHY, Michael.
NULTY, Edmund.
OSBORNE, Marcus Stuart,
  Rosnaree.
REGAN, Paul, Brownstown,
  Beauparc.

SOUTHWELL, Thomas.
VAUGHEY, John.

Stamullin

CARR, Patrick.
CLARKE, Lawrence.
DOMEGAN, Christopher Patrick,
  Ardcath.
GOUGH, Patrick.
HAMILTON, Andrew, Ardcath.
JAMESON, Edward.
McKEON, James.
RUSSELL, William Francis.
WALSH, Edward.
WADE, George Edward.

Summerhill

BARNARD, William.
FARRELL, Philip.
ROBINSON, Charles.
ROWLEY, The Hon. George Cecil.
SMYTH, Matthew.
WALSH, Michael.

Trim

ALLEN, John.
BEHAN, Thomas.
BIRD, Michael.
BROGAN, William Bernard.
CARROLL, Christopher.
CHAMBERS, Edward Chandos
  Elliott.

CLARKE, Patrick.
CONNOR, James.
CONNORS, Joseph.
COX, Patrick.
CROSBY, Hugh.
ENNIS, Michael.
FARRELL, Paul.
FAUGHLIN, Patrick.
FINNEGAN, Thomas.
FORAN, John.
GAUGHRAN, Christopher.
GIBBONS, Patrick.
GIBNEY, John.
GOGARTY, Christopher.
GRIFFITH, George.
HALLIGAN, John.
HALLIGAN, Richard.
HALTON, Matthew, Clonfane.
McCORMACK, Henry.
McGUIRE, Andrew.
McGUIRE, William.
McMANUS, James.
MALONE, William.
MOONEY, Michael.
MURPHY, George.
MURRAY, John, Kildalkey.
NUGENT, Thomas.
NULTY, Patrick.
O'BRIEN, Gerald.
O'DARE, James.
O'DARE, John.
POTTERTON, William Hubert.
PURDON, George Hardress.
QUINN, Peter.
REGAN, Matthew J.
REILLY, James.
REYNOLDS, Peter.
ROCHFORD, Joseph.

ROCHFORD, Michael.
ROE, Joseph.
ROGERS, James.
SMYTH, William.
STONES, Pat.
WYLLIE, James.

Wilkinstown and Castletown

DUFFY, Thomas, Castletown.
GILLIAT, Cecil ("Glennie")
  Glendower Percival, Arch Hall,
  Wilkinstown.
GILLIATT, Reginald Horace
  Crosbie, Arch Hall, Wilkinstown.
GILSENAN, Thomas, Kilberry.
KELLY, Joseph, Wilkinstown.
KIERAN, James, Castletown.

McCANN, Joseph, Kilberry.
MEEHAN, Patrick, Wilkinstown
MEGAN, Lawrence, Wilkinstown.
MOORE, John, Wilkinstown.

Addresses in Meath but no clear address

CONNOLLY, James, Moate, Co.
  Meath.
CONNORTON, W., Meath.
McGUINNESS, Michael, Meath.
McKENNA, Denis, Meath.
MILLS, R.S., Meath.
MURTAGH, James, Meath.
PAGE, Henry George, Meath.
REILLY, Michael, Meath.
ROURKE, John, Meath.

Sources and Further Information

Michael McGoona, Meath Great War Dead, *Meath Chronicle*, 31 July and 7 August 2004

A.J. Horneck, *Roll of Honour*, (Navan, 1916).

Ireland's Memorial Record, World War I, 1914-1918

Marquis de Ruvigny's *The Roll of Honour, 1914-1924: A Biographical Record of Members of His Majesty's Naval and Military Forces who Fell in the Great War*

Donal Hall, *The Unreturned Army County Louth Dead in the Great War 1914-1918* (Dundalk, 2005)

Meath Chronicle

Drogheda Independent

National Archives, Kew Medal Lists

National Archives, Service Records

Soldiers Died in the Great War, 1914-1919

Commonwealth War Graves Commission.

David Robertson, *Deeds not Words: Irish Soldiers, Sailors and Airmen of Two World Wars* (Multyfarnham, 1998)

Library and Archives, Canada.

Australian Service Records

Census 1901 and 1911

Parish Registers